최신 토익 RC 수험서

핵심 토익 RC

박현석 著

21세기사

서 문

　　지금도 많은 학생들이 취업에 필요한 토익 점수를 위해 매일 매일 땀을 흘리고 있으리라 생각한다. 최근에 토익 과목 문제가 바뀌어 새로운 문제에 대한 대비가 필요하게 되었다. 영어 자체가 공부하기에 시간과 인내를 요하는 과목이어서 수험생들의 부담이 큰 것만은 사실이지만 핵심적인 내용을 잘 정리하고 문제를 풀어본다면 좋은 결과를 얻을 수 있으리라 생각한다.

　　이에 저자는 대학에서 취업공부를 하고 있는 대학생을 가르쳐온 경험을 바탕으로 토익 시험에 꼭 필요한 내용만을 엄선하여 다음과 같이 본서를 출간하게 되었다.

　PART Ⅰ : 영문법 중에서 필수적인 내용만을 10장으로 정리하였고, 이 내용을 중심으로 토익 기본문제, 토익 실전문제를 풀어봄으로써 영문법에 자신감을 갖도록 다양한 문제를 수록하였다.

　PART Ⅱ : 최근에 어휘문제가 상당히 까다롭게 출제되고 있어 기본 단어를 정리해 놓았고, 다양한 어휘 문제를 풀어보도록 어휘 문제를 엄선해서 정리해 놓았다.

　PART Ⅲ : 토익 독해를 풀 수 있는 기본적인 독해 요령을 정리해 놓았고 토익 독해문제 part 6 와 part 7 문제를 수록하여 최근 출제경향을 파악하도록 하였다.

　PART Ⅳ : 문법, 어휘, 독해를 공부한 후에 자신의 실력을 테스트해 보도록 토익 모의고사 문제 100 문항을 수록하였다.

　　끝으로 이 책을 흔쾌히 출판해 주신 21세기 출판사 이 범만 사장님께 깊은 감사를 드리며 학생들이 이 책을 통해 여러분의 취업에 일조를 한다면 필자에게 더 없이 큰 기쁨이 될 것입니다.

저자 박 현 석

목 차 (Contents)

Part 1 토익 영문법

Part 2 토익 어휘

Part 3 토익 독해

Part 4 토익(RC) 실전 문제 (100문제)

◎ 신 토익 시험의 구성

구성	Part	문제유형	문항 수	문항 구성	시간 및 배점
Listening Comprehension	1	사진묘사	6		45분/495점
	2	질의응답	25		
	3	2인/3인 대화	39	13개 대화/3문항씩	
	4	1인 담화	30	10개 담화/3문항씩	
Reading Comprehension	5	단문 공란 메우기	30		75분/495점
	6	장문 공란 메우기	16	4개 지문/4문항씩	
	7	한 개 지문	29	10개 지문/2~4문항씩	
		두 개 지문	10	2개 지문/5문항씩	
		세 개 지문	15	3개 지문/5문항씩	
Total	7 Parts		200		120분/990점

[1] PART 5 / 단문 공란 메우기(30문항)

1. **문제 유형**: 빈칸이 포함된 단문이 주어지고, 4개의 선택지 중에서 빈칸에 알맞은 것을 고르는 문제이다.

   (ex) Mattie White is going to lead a _____ on the new marketing policies this afternoon. (①)

   ① workshop   ② meaning   ③ rule   ④ model

2. **시간 배분**: Reading Comprehension을 푸는데 주어진 시간은 총 75분이다. 장문으로 이루어진 Part 6와 Part 7에서 충분한 시간을 확보하려면 Part5에서는 12분을 넘기지 않도록 해야 한다.

3. **출제 포인트**: 문법, 문장구조, 어휘 세 가지를 주로 묻는다.

(1) **문법:** 특정한 문법적 지식을 알고 있는지를 묻고 있지만 어떤 문제는 복합적인 문법지식을 테스트하기도 한다.

> (ex) Vegetables _____ they bought in the Roger's Supermarket are cheaper than others. (①)
>
> ① that ② what ③ who ④ than

(2) **문장구조:** 빈칸에 들어갈 단어의 적절한 품사를 묻는 경우가 대부분으로, 각기 다른 품사로 선택지가 구성되어 있다.

> (ex) This morning, the manager called Ms. Gomez into his office and for her _____. (④)
>
> ① advise ② advised ③ advisable ④ advice

(3) **어휘:** 다양한 어휘의 뜻을 얼마나 확실히 알고 있는지를 묻는다. 개별 단어의 의미를 문제부터 2차 의미나, 어법을 묻는 문제도 가끔 출제된다.

> (ex) Send all the _____ in this company an e-mail about the conversation plans. (②)
>
> ① jobs ② workers ③ profits ④ tools

4. **신 토익 전략:** 신 토익문제에서는 독해비중이 증가하고 Part5 문제 수가 감소함에 따라 문법이 비중이 줄었다고 착각할 수 있지만 여전히 Part6 & Part7에서도 문법적인 내용을 상당수 묻고 있으므로 기본적인 문법지식이 필요하다. Part5에서 문제를 빨리 풀어 Part6 & Part7을 위한 시간을 확보하는 연습이 필요하다.

[2] PART 6 / 장문 공란 메우기(16문항)

1. **문제 유형:** 지문 하나당 4개의 문항이 출제되고, 각 문항은 Part 5처럼 4개의 선택지 중 빈칸에 알맞은 것을 고르는 문제이다. Part5처럼 문법, 문장구조, 어휘를 묻는 문제이지만, 지문 속에서 전체 맥락을 통해 문제 정답을 고르는 문제도 출제된다. 특히 신 토익에서는 단순히 어휘가 아닌 빈칸에 적절한 문장을 찾는 문제가 새롭게 출제되므로 글의 흐름을 파악하는 노력이 필요하다 하겠다.

2. **시간 배분:** 16문제를 최대한 8분 안에 해결하도록 하고 남은 시간을 Part 7에 할애하는 시간관리가 필요하다.

3. **출제 포인트:** 빈칸이 지문 중간에 들어가 있지만, 출제 포인트 및 선택지 구성은 Part 5와 같다. 단, 장문에서 출제되므로 빈칸이 있는 해당문제만 봐도 해결되는 문제가 있는 반면, 앞뒤 맥락을 통해 정답을 가려내야 하는 까다로운 문제도 출제된다. 특히 새롭게 추가된 '빈칸에 알맞은 문장을 고르는 유형'은 앞뒤 문맥에서 정답을 추론해야 하므로 문장 전체를 빨리 이해하는 독해실력이 더욱 중요해졌다.

4. **신 토익 전략:** 기존에는 Part 5가 장문이긴 했으나 빈칸 문장 혹은 앞뒤 문장만 내용을 파악하면 되므로 Part 5와 유사하게 문법 및 어휘문제가 출제되고 있다. 하지만 '빈칸에 알맞은 문장을 고르는 유형'이 추가됨에 따라 Part 7처럼 독   해실력이 더욱 필요해졌다. 따라서 단순히 빈칸 주변 보다는 앞뒤 문맥이나 전체문맥을 파악해야 풀 수 있는 문제가 더 많아진 것이다. 또한 빈칸 밑에 바로 선택지가 있었던 문제 유형에서 지문과 선택지가 분리되는 형태로 바뀜에 따라, 빈칸과 선택지를 빠르게 봐야하는 훈련도 필요해진 결과를 가져왔다.

[3] PART 7 / 독해(54문항)

1. **문제 유형:** 주어진 지문을 읽고 제시된 2~5개의 질문에 답하는 문제유형이다. 총 54문제가 출제되는데 각 지문의 종류별 문항 수는 다음과 같다.

지문 종류	지문 수	지문 당 문항 수	전체 문항 수
한 개의 지문	10개	2~4 문항	20개
두 개의 지문	2개	5 문항	10개
세 개의 지문	3개	5 문항	15개

2. **시간배분:** 수험생들이 시간 부족을 가장 많이 호소하는 부분이 바로 Part 7이다. 긴 지문을 읽고 풀어야 하기 때문에 소요되는 시간이 많이 걸리기 때문이다.

3. **출제 포인트**

   A. **지문 종류**

   (1) **한 개의 지문:** 편지, e-mail, 공지문, 메모, 광고, 기사문, 설명서 등 다양한 양식의 문제가 출제된다. 신 토익에서는 실제 생활에 많이 등장하는 지문을 제시하고 문자 메시지나 채팅 대화문과 같은 SNS 관련 지문이 추가되었다.

   (2) **두 개의 지문:** 공지나 메모에 대한 답신, 편지나 e-mail에 대한 답신, 공지문과 청구내역 등 서로 연관된 지문들이 출제된다.

   (3) **세 개의 지문:** 광고를 보고 주문을 했는데 주문이 잘못되어 항의 하는 e-mail을 보내는 등 서로 연관성이 있는 세 개의 지문이 출제된다. 세 개의 지문이 출제되지 만 두 개의 지문과 비슷한 유형으로 보면 된다.

   B. **문제 유형:** 일반적인 정보(글의 주제, 목적, 출처 등)의 구체적인 정보를 묻는 문제로 나누어진다. 대부분 한 지문 당 일반적인 정보를 묻는

문제는 하나만 출제되고 나머지는 모두 구체적인 정보를 묻는 문제가 출제된다. 특히 신 토익에서는 Part 7에서 출제되는 '화자의 의도를 묻는 유형' 과 '문장의 적절한 위치를 묻는 유형' 이 추가되어 새로운 문제 유형에 대한 대비가 필요하다.

C. 패러프레이징 (paraphrasing: 의역): 패러프레이징이란 어떤 내용을 다른 말로 바꾸어 표현하는 것을 말한다. 토익에서는 지문에 등장하는 표현을 질문이나 선택지에서 다르게 표현하여 출제한다. 이렇게 패러프레이징하는 이유는 내용을 잘 이해했는지를 평가하기 위해서이다.

4. 신 토익 대비: 신 토익의 가장 큰 특징은 독해영역의 비중이 늘어난 것이다. 독해는 영어의 기초가 부족한 수험생들이 어려워하는 영역이고 단기간에 점수를 올리기 힘들기 때문에 가장 힘든 부분이 될 수 있다. 독해를하는 데 가장 중요한 것은 문장을 읽는데 어휘와 독해 스킬을 연습하는 것이다. 시간이 걸리더라도 꾸준히 독해분량을 늘려가면서 훈련하는 것이 필요하다. 이를 위해 평소 토익에 자주 출제되는 지문의 유형을 파악해 둔다면 지문을 풀어가는 데 훨씬 수월할 것이다.

Part 1 ··· 토 익 영 문 법

문장 구조

(1) 문장의 5형식

❶ **1형식**(S + V 문형): 「주어+동사」만으로 완전한 의미를 나타낼 수 있으며, 수식어로 부사(구)가 붙을 수 있다.

(ex) ① Birds sing joyfully.　② The earth moves round the sun.

③ My uncle in Seoul works at a bank.

④ There is a bench under the tree.

⑤ Many years ago a large fox lived in the woods.

❷ **2형식**(S + V + C 문형): 보어가 필요한 동사⇒ 동사만으로는 주어에 대한 설명이 부족하여 주격보어를 필요로 하는 불완전 자동사(be, seem, remain/ smell, taste, look, feel, sound 등의 감각 동사)가 있는 문장이다. 주격보어가 될 수 있는 것은 명사(=부정사, 동명사, 대명사), 형용사(=분사)등이다.

(ex) ① He is a tough guy.　② Mary is beautiful.

③ My hobby is collecting(=to collect) stamps.

④ The gates remained closed for years.　⑤ He looks pale.

❸ **3형식**(S + V + O 문형): 목적어를 필요로 하는 타동사가 있는 문장으로 우리말로 ~를(을)」로 해석이 되며, 목적어가 될 수 있는 것은 명사(구), 대명사, 부정사, 동명사 등이 있다.

(ex) ① He married a beautiful lady. ② I have finished writing a letter.

③ They helped him yesterday. ④ Do you know how to drive a car?

*3형식 동사: 자동사로 착각하기 쉬운 타동사: 전치사 없이 바로 뒤에 목적어가 온다. (enter, attend, marry, discuss, mention, approach 등)

(ex) ① Judy married a handsome man yesterday.

② We discussed this problem.

*3형식 동사: 4형식으로 착각하기 쉬운 타동사: explain, introduce

(ex) I introduced my sister to my friend.

* I introduced my friend my sister. (틀림)

❹ **4형식**(S + V + I.O + D.O 문형): 「~에게 ~를」 주었다 처럼 2개의 목적어를 갖는 수여동사로 give, teach, tell, send, show, write/ buy/ ask 등의 동사이다.

(ex) ① He gave me the book. (=He gave the book to me.)

② Father bought me a camera. (=Father bought a camera for me.)

❺ **5형식**(S + V + O + C 문형): 목적어의 상태, 동작을 설명해주는 목적보어를 필요로 하는 불완전 타동사가 이끄는 문장으로, 목적보어는 명사, 형용사, 분사, 부정사, 원형부정사 등이 나올 수 있다.

(ex) ① He made his son a doctor.   ② I called him a fool.

③ I made her happy.   ④ Tom found the book easy.

⑤ I ordered him to stay.   ⑥ I saw Mary cross (crossing) the street.

⑦ I heard my name called by Tom.

(2) 주의해야 될 동사

① Illness *prevented* him *from* going. (~때문에 ~할 수 없다)

[keep, prohibit, hinder, deter, ban] + 사람 + from + V-ing

② He can distinguish(=tell) the right from the wrong. (A와 B를 구별하다)

③ His troubles deprived(robbed) him of sleep. (A로부터 B를 빼앗다)

토익 기본 문제

※ Choose the best form of the underlined parts. (1~9)

01 _____,the company attained economic independence.

① Within a year ② A year ③ A year has passed ④ As a year

02 The police _____the area near our company.

① to patrol ② patrol ③ patrolling ④ to have patrolled

03 A newspaper _____us in touch with the world.

① keeping ② to keep ③ keeps ④ keep

04 Check-out time _____1:00 p.m.

① at ② when ③ or ④ is

05 _____penguins in the Arctic.

① There are no ② There is not ③ No ④ All

06 Because of his illness he had to _____his job.

① quit ② quit from ③ to quit ④ quitting

07 I never feel very _____when I walk about that street.

① safely ② safety ③ safe ④ save

08 I had my composition _____by our professor.

① corrected ② correct ③ corrective ④ correcting

09 The faculty meeting _____every night at 7:oo p.m.

① began ② begin ③ beginning ④ begins

토익 실전 문제

※ Choose the best form of the underlined parts. (1~10)

01 During the trial period, please _____ the new employee's progress carefully.

① monitors   ② monitor   ③ monitoring   ④ monitored

02 Under the new policy, _____ for full-time employees is determined solely by performance.

① compensatory   ② compensated
③ compensation   ④ compensates

03 The _____ laptop from Vida Co. received favorable reviews for its lightweight.

① frequent   ② innovative   ③ estimated   ④ reluctant

04 The new tracking system _____ the warehouse to ship goods more efficiently.

① will allow   ② to allow   ③ allowance   ④ allowing

05 Some of the vehicle's _____ should be replaced because they are worn.

① capacities   ② specifications   ③ procedures   ④ components

06 Office supply purchases that exceed $100 require _____ from the finance department.

① approved   ② approval   ③ approving   ④ approve

07 The maintenance crew regularly trims the park's bushes so that the walking paths are clearly _____.

① visibly   ② visibility   ③ vision   ④ visible

08 Experienced technicians _____ the laboratory equipment carefully before an experiment begins.

① perform   ② function   ③ revise   ④ inspect

09 When checking in for your flight , please state your _____ for the smoking or the non-smoking section.

① preference   ② prefer   ③ preferably   ④ preferential

10 You had better purchase the house where you can feel _____

① comfort   ② comfortable   ③ comfortably   ④ comforter

[정답]

1	2	3	4	5	6	7	8	9
①	②	③	④	①	①	④	①	④

1	2	3	4	5	6	7	8	9	10
②	③	②	①	④	②	④	④	①	②

시제

```
                                                    ┌─────────────────────┐
                                                    │      미래완료        │
                                                    │  현재→미래의 기간    │
                          ┌──────────────┬──────────────┐
                          │   과거완료    │   현재완료    │
                          │ 대과거→과거의 기간 │ 과거→현재의 기간 │
                          │              │              │
                    ─────┼──────────────┼──────────────┼──────────────
                          │   과거진행    │   현재진행    │   미래진행
    ══════════════════════════════════════════════════════════════════
       대과거            과거           현재           미래
                         (한            (한 시점)      (한
   (과거 이전의 시점)    시점)                          시점)
```

(1) 기본시제: 현재, 과거, 미래 시제가 있다.

a) 현재 시제의 용법
 ① 현재의 사실: (ex) He lives in Mokpo.
 ② 현재 반복되는 습관: (ex) She always goes to church every Sunday.
 ③ 불변의 진리: (ex) The earth moves round the sun.
 ④ 미래의 대용: 때나 조건을 나타내는 부사절에서 미래의 의미를 현재 시제로
　　　　　　　　표현한다.
　　　　　　　(ex) I will study, *if it rains tomorrow.*
　　　　　　　　　　Let's wait *until he comes.*
　　　　　　(주의) Please tell me *when he will arrive there.*
　　　☞왕래·발착동사는 현재형이나, 현재 진행형으로 가까운 미래를 표시함.
　　　(ex) We start tomorrow. We are starting tomorrow.

b) 과거 시제의 용법
　① 과거의 사실: 보통, in+과거 연도, ~ago, last~ 등의 표현과 같이 쓰인다.
　　(ex) He visited the city two years ago. I met her yesterday.
　② 과거의 습관: (ex) Sun-hee used to take a walk early in the morning.
　③ 역사적 사실: (ex) The Korean War broke out in 1950.

c) 미래 시제의 용법: 미래에 일어날 사건이나 상태를 나타냄

(2) 현재완료 시제 (현재완료는 과거와 현재를 연결시켜 주는 시제)

용법	내　용	예　문
완료	주로 부사 <u>just</u> 와 함께 쓰임	He has just arrived.(just는 과거형과도 사용됨)
경험	주로 빈도부사인 often, once, ~times, ever등과 쓰임	Have you ever seen D.J.?
		Yes, I′ve seen him once before.
계속	주로 for, <u>since</u>와 함께 쓰임	Mary has known the fact since two days ago.
		He has been in the army for two years. (=He is still in the army.)
결과	과거에 행한 동작의 결과가 현재까지 남아있음	I bought a watch.(내가 과거에 시계를 샀는데, 지금도 가지고 있는가는 알 수 없음.)
		I have bought a watch.(내가 과거에 시계를 사서 지금도 확실히 가지고 있음.)

(3) 진행시제: Be + V~ing(현재분사)

① I <u>will be studying</u> English.　② I <u>am studying</u> English.

③ I <u>was studying</u> English.　　④ I <u>have been studying</u> English.

[동사 불규칙 변화 20개]

	동사원형	과거형	과거분사		동사원형	과거형	과거분사
1	begin	began	begun	11	send	sent	sent
2	draw	drew	drawn	12	build	built	built
3	eat	ate	eaten	13	sing	sang	sung
4	feel	felt	felt	14	swim	swam	swum
5	forget	forgot	forgotten	15	teach	taught	taught
6	make	made	made	16	tell	told	told
7	take	took	taken	17	think	thought	thought
8	awake	awoke	awoke	18	throw	threw	thrown
9	do	did	done	19	meet	met	met
10	see	saw	seen	20	know	knew	known

토익 기본 문제

※ Choose the best form of the underlined parts. (1~9)

01 The company fired many employees _____.

　① for two years　② since two years　③ two years ago　④ in two years

02 The earth _____ around the sun.

　① move　② will move　③ moved　④ moves

03 She _____ the place three times.

　① has visited　② went　③ goes　④ have visited

04 He _____ his girlfriend at the restaurant yesterday.

　① meets　② has met　③ meet　④ met

05 The legislature will adjourn as soon as they _____ on the budget proposal.

　① will vote　② vote　③ voted　④ have voted

06 I _____ George Smith for several years.

　① know　② knows　③ has known　④ have known

07 Sun-hee _____ to church every Sunday.

　① go　② will　③ goes　④ went

08 The businessmen always _____ to their favorite restaurant for lunch.

　① go　② went　③ will go　④ has gone

09 If it _____ in the afternoon, the flight to New York will have to be canceled.

　① rains　② will rain　③ would rain　④ rain

토익 실전 문제

※ Choose the best form of the underlined parts. (1~10)

01 With great excitement, Mr. Thomson _____ yesterday that the company's stocks are at an all-time high.

① announce ② announces ③ announcing ④ announced

02 Risk management specialists _____ what the company can do to avoid losses.

① purchase ② move ③ determine ④ confess

03 Over the next couple of weeks, the Festival Theater _____ auditions for its newest play.

① held ② has held ③ will hold ④ had been holding

04 Government agencies _____ check the quality of the city's drinking water.

① regularly ② yet ③ recently ④ formerly

05 By the time his next novel is released, Juan Fuentes _____ five books for young adults.

① published ② has published ③ will have published ④ is publishing

06 Managers will review over 100 resumes before the interview process _____.

① beginning ② begins ③ begin ④ began

07 Hanto Electronics, Inc., plans to _____ Dobby Digital Company because of its successful range of digital cameras.

① arrive ② perform ③ generate ④ acquire

08 Residents say that the construction _____ an increase in traffic for the past few weeks.

① will cause   ② is causing   ③ has caused   ④ causes

09 I'll have to call picnic off if it _____ tomorrow.

① rains   ② rained   ③ will rain   ④ would rain

10 Three years _____ since his mother died.

① passed   ② has passed   ③ had passed   ④ have passed

[정답]

1	2	3	4	5	6	7	8	9
③	②	④	③	③	③	④	①	③

1	2	3	4	5	6	7	8	9	10
④	③	③	①	③	②	④	③	①	④

수동태

능동태	수동태
목적어 ↔	주 어
타동사 ↔	be+p.p
주 어 ↔	by+목적격
▶ 나머지 부분은 뒤에 그대로 이어 쓰면 됨	

수동태의 시제 변화
① 단순시제 : 「be+p.p」
② 완료시제 : 「have [has;had] +been+p.p」
③ 진행시제 : 「be+being+p.p」
④ 부정시제 : 「be+not+p.p」
⑤ 조 동 사 : 「조동사+be+p.p」

(1) 수동태를 만드는 기본 공식

① 3형식: S   V   O →

O   be+p.p   by+S

(ex) They built the house in 1995.

→ The house was built in 1995 by them.

② 「목적어」가 명사절(that)인 경우: 가주어 it를 사용

(ex) They say that he is happy.

→ It is said that he is happy (by them).

→ He is said to be happy (by them).

③ 동사구의 수동: 동사구는 붙어 다닌다.

(ex) He took care of his brother.

→ His brother was taken care of by him.

④ 수여동사의 수동: 목적어가 두 개 있으므로 수동태가 두 개 가능

(ex) John gave her the report.

→ ⓐ The report was given (to) her by John.

ⓑ She was given the report by John.

⑤ 지각동사와 사역동사의 수동: 능동문의 원형부정사가 to-부정사로 바뀐다.

(ex) ⓐ We heard her talk with her friends.

→ She was heard to talk with her friends by us.

ⓑ We made him enter the office.

→ He was made to enter the office by us.

⑥ by 대신에 다른 전치사를 쓰는 동사

(ex) ⓐ The news surprised me.

→ I *was surprised at* the news.(~에 놀라다)

ⓑ I *was pleased with* the result.(~로 기뻐하다)

ⓒ I *am concerned about* my health.(~를 염려하다)

ⓓ I *am interested in* the job.(~에 흥미 있다)

ⓔ The accident *was known to* everyone. (~에게 알려져 있다)

ⓕ He *is known as* a politician.(~로 유명하다)

ⓖ be covered with / be graduated from

⑦ have (get) + O + p.p: (시키다, 당하다)

(ex) I have my purse stolen.

⑧ 조동사가 있는 수동태: 조동사를 그대로 사용한다.

(ex) You must solve the problem.

→ The problem must be solved by you.

토익 기본 문제

※ Choose the best form of the underlined parts. (1~9)

01 Taking photographs _____ in this building.

① can not allow ② has not permission ③ is not allowed ④ doesn't allow

02 The city is run _____ a mayor.

① to ② by ③ from ④ with

03 _____ that people should learn to dive when they are learning how to swim.

① Believing ② To believe ③ They are believed ④ It is believed

04 I was surprised _____ the news.

① by ② to ③ at ④ from

05 A telephone _____ in your office next week.

① installed ② will install ③ will be installed ④ installs

06 Strangely enough, Mr. Taylor was not seen _____ his house last night.

① enter ② being entered ③ to enter ④ having entered

07 All people in the world are interested _____ the games of World Cup.

① by ② with ③ at ④ in

08 A great deal of pleasure and satisfaction _____ in this task.

① can be found ② can find ③ can be founded ④ can found

09 People _____ that Dr. Lee's son is very excellent.

① are said ② is said ③ say ④ is saying

토익 실전 문제

※ Choose the best form of the underlined parts. (1~10)

01 Until the hotel's recreational area has been _____, guests are prohibited from using.

① renovate   ② renovating   ③ renovation   ④ renovated

02 An expanded parking garage _____under Ms. Swenson's uptown office building.

① is located   ② located   ③ are being located   ④ was locating

03 In light of the national recall, customers _____any Gilmore product without proof   of purchase.

① to be returned   ② may return   ③ returning   ④ should be returned

04 Elaine Sturrock has recently been _____to head of personal at Bacary Pharmaceuticals, Inc.

① applied   ② agreed   ③ promoted   ④ tried

05 Business First U.K. _____the best nonprofit group for assisting entrepreneurs.

① considered   ② is considered   ③ consider   ④ to consider

06 Since last year, most of the negotiations with our partners _____by Bogart International.

① will be conducted   ② have conducted
③ have been conducted   ④ was conducting

07 Sherman and Lopez's law team is_____to providing exceptional legal advice.

① serious   ② distributed   ③ supportable   ④ dedicated

08 The winner of the presidential election _____promptly at 6 o'clock tomorrow night.

① is announcing   ② has been announced

③ will announce   ④ will be announced

09 Dentists agree that brushing your teeth three times a day _____good dental health and a more attractive smile.

① promote   ② promotes   ③ to promote   ④ was promoted

10 Every boy and girl _____invited to the meeting.

① were   ② was   ③ have   ④ has

[정답]

1	2	3	4	5	6	7	8	9
③	②	④	③	③	③	④	①	③

1	2	3	4	5	6	7	8	9	10
④	①	②	③	③	③	④	④		

 **일 치**

(1) 주어와 동사의 일치

: 주어와 동사는 수가 일치해야 되는데 주어가 수식어구로 분리된 경우와 상관접속사로 연결된 경우에 유의해야 한다.

① A and B가 불가분의 관계인 경우는 단수 취급.

(ex) <u>Curry and rice</u> <u>is</u> my usual lunch.   <u>Slow and steady</u> <u>wins</u> the race.

② 유도부사인 there는 주어가 동사 뒤에 온다.

(ex) There <u>is</u> <u>a book</u> on the table.   There <u>are</u> <u>many books</u> on the table.

③ every 와 each로 연결된 명사는 항상 단수 취급.

(ex) <u>Every</u> boy and girl <u>was</u> invited to the meeting.(○)
      <u>Every</u> boy and girl <u>were</u> invited to the meeting.(×)

④ 상관접속사인 both A and B 는 항상 복수 취급.

(ex) <u>Both</u> English <u>and</u> politics <u>are</u> my favorite subject.

⑤ A as well as B 는 A에, not only A but also B는 B에 동사를 일치시킨다.

(ex) <u>I</u> <u>as well as</u> he <u>am</u> interested in English.
      <u>Not only</u> he <u>but also</u> <u>I am</u> interested in English.

⑥ neither A nor B; either A or B; not A but B는 B에 동사를 일치시킨다.

(ex) <u>Either</u> you <u>or</u> I am in the wrong.
      <u>Not</u> I <u>but</u> <u>they were</u> punished.

⑦ the number of + 복수명사는 단수로, a number of + 복수명사는 복수로 취급한다.

(ex) <u>The number of</u> students <u>is</u> forty.
      <u>A number of</u> students <u>are</u> absent from school.

⑧ 시간, 가격, 거리등을 표시하는 복수형 명사를 한 단어로 취급하는 경우 단수 취급
한다.

(ex) Eighty years seems to be a long lifetime.

⑨ 한 쌍으로 된 물건은 항상 복수 취급한다. [glasses, scissors, binoculars]

(ex) My scissors need sharpening.

⑩ 학문명, 병명 그리고 news 등은 복수형이지만 항상 단수 취급한다.

(ex) Bad news travels quickly. Electronics is difficult to learn.

(2) 관계대명사의 선행사와 동사의 일치

: 관계대명사가 주격인 경우, 동사는 선행사의 수에 일치해야 한다.

(ex) He is the only one of my friends who really likes me.

(3) 인칭대명사는 앞에 나온 명사의 수에 일치

(ex) A dog bit the man who was trying to kick at it.

I asked the women on what they based their predictions.

(4) 지시대명사의 일치: 단수명사 (it, its, it)/ 복수명사 (they, their, them)

토익 기본 문제

※ Choose the best form of the underlined parts. (1~9)

01 It is a message of importance for every man and woman who _____ .

① votes　　② vote　　③ voting　　④ are vote

02 Advertisements on TV _____ becoming more competitive than ever before.

① is　　② are　　③ has　　④ have

03 There _____ some people at the meeting last night.

① are　　② is　　③ were　　④ was

04 Neither Jill nor her parents _____ seen this movie before.

① has　　② have　　③ is　　④ are

05 Although many people regard whales as fish, _____ mammals.

① it is　　② it has　　③ they are　　④ they have

06 Physics _____ his favorite subject.

① is　　② are　　③ has　　④ have

07 Bread and butter _____ all he ate.

① is　　② are　　③ was　　④ were

08 The United States _____ a big country.

① is　　② are　　③ has　　④ have

09 Your glasses _____ on the table last night.

① is　　② are　　③ was　　④ were

토익 실전 문제

※ Choose the best form of the underlined parts. (1~10)

01 Successful installation of the new security cameras _____ the help of a professional.

① to require   ② require   ③ requires   ④ requiring

02 Salary _____ are based on the employee's work history and performance.

① increasingly   ② increasing   ③ increase   ④ increases

03 Even though Mr. Wilkie lacks technical _____ in his field, he decided not to attend the skills workshop.

① impression   ② expense   ③ indication   ④ expertise

04 Orders submitted on Friday _____ processed the following week on Monday.

① are   ② is   ③ being   ④ to be

05 Shin Manufacturing, Inc., requests that its more _____ workers assist new recruits whenever necessary.

① flexible   ② previous   ③ temporary   ④ experienced

06 Martin Lewis provides excellent customer service to clients and fully _____ a raise.

① deservedly   ② deserve   ③ deserves   ④ deserving

07 Nearly 500 people from all over the country _____ for the annual conference on environmental studies.

① register   ② registers   ③ has registered   ④ is registering

08 Leading _____ agree that it is possible to develop an environmentally friendly fuel.

① chemist   ② chemists   ③ chemical   ④ chemically

09 Dentists agree that brushing your teeth three times a day _____ good dental health and a more attractive smile.

① promote   ② promotes   ③ to promote   ④ was promoted

10 Every boy and girl _____ invited to the meeting.

① were   ② was   ③ have   ④ has

[정답]

1	2	3	4	5	6	7	8	9
①	②	③	④	③	①	③	①	④

1	2	3	4	5	6	7	8	9	10
③	④	④	①	④	③	①	②	②	②

부정사

영어에서 다양한 표현을 하기 위해 동사의 형태를 약간 변형시켜 원래는 품사가 동사지만 실제 문장에서는 다른 품사로 쓰이는 동사 형태.

준동사 종류	형 태	품사변화
(1) 부정사	to+V	명사, 형용사, 부사
(2) 동명사	V+-ing	명사
(3) 분 사	V+-ing (현재분사) V+-ed (과거분사)	형용사

(1) 부정사 용법

a) 명사적 용법: 문장의 주어, 보어, 목적어로 사용된다.

　(ex) To stop smoking is very hard. (= It is very hard to stop smoking.)

　　　My dream in future is to be a famous comedian.

　　　He decided to go there with us. (want, hope, wish, expect, promise, demand)

b) 형용사적 용법: 명사 바로 뒤에서 앞의 명사를 수식하거나 목적보어로 사용된다.

　(ex) He was the first person to come here. I consider John to be honest.

c) 부사적 용법: 주로 목적으로 사용되며 원인, 결과, 조건, 이유로 사용 가능

용 법	해 석	예 문
목 적	~하기 위해서	He ran to catch the bus.
원 인	~해서	I am very glad to meet you again. (sorry, happy)
이 유	~하다니	He must be mad to say so. (cannot be)
조 건	~한다면	To turn to the left, you will find a postman.
결 과	~해보니 ~하다	I awoke to find myself famous.
형용사 수식	~하기에	French is hard to learn.

(2) 부정사를 목적보어로 취하는 동사

want, expect, cause, enable, force, tell, ask, allow, permit, warn, forbid

order, compel + 목적어 (사람) + to V (hope 동사는 안됨)

(ex) I want him to finish the work by tomorrow.   *I <u>hope</u> you <u>to do</u> it. (틀림)

(3) 원형부정사의 용법

① 지각동사 (see, hear, feel, watch) + O + O.C (원형부정사)

   (ex) I saw him enter the house.

      (= He was seen to enter the house by me.)

② 사역동사 (have, make, let) + O + O.C (원형부정사)

   (ex) Father made me turn off the radio.

③ 준 사역동사(=help): (ex) Doctors help sick people (to) live better lives.

   (부정사, 원형부정사 둘 다 가능)

(4) 부정사의 의미상의 주어

의미상 주어 형태	용 법	예 문
for+의미상 주어	일반 형용사	The clothes are too small for me to wear.
of+의미상 주어	stupid, nice, kind, wise, sensible	It is kind of you to help me.
5형식 문장	목적어	I expect you to pass the exam.
생략	일반 사람	It is wrong (for you) to tell a lie.

(5) 부정사의 시제: 주절과 종속절의 시제가 동일하면 단순형, 다르면 완료형을 사용

① 단순 부정사 (to+V): (ex) She seems to be sick. (=It <u>seems</u> that she <u>is</u> sick.)

② 완료 부정사 (to have + p.p)

   (ex) He seems to have been sick. (=It <u>seems</u> that he <u>was</u> sick.)

(6) 관용 표현: ① 『enough to V』 : (ex) He is old enough to go to school.

                  (= He is so old that he can go to school.)

               ② 『too~to V』 : (ex) This coffee is too hot for us to drink.

                  (=This coffee is so hot that we can't drink it.)

토익 기본 문제

※ Choose the best form of the underlined parts. (1~9)

01 I decided _____ money, because I needed a lot of money to live in Korea.

① to save   ② saving   ③ saved   ④ have saved

02 America is the best place for anyone who _____ English.

① practicing   ② practiced   ③ to be practiced   ④ to practice

03 It is very hard _____ smoking.

① stop   ② to stop   ③ stopping   ④ stopped

04 Father made me _____ the radio.

① turned off   ② turning off   ③ to turn off   ④ turn off

05 It is very stupid _____ to do such a thing.

① of you   ② for you   ③ that you   ④ you

06 They are negotiating a land purchase _____ a new company.

① to build   ② for build   ③ build   ④ builds

07 I'd be happy _____ you in my car.

① for taking   ② taken   ③ to take   ④ taking

08 The bad weather yesterday made them _____ the company picnic.

① postpone   ② postponed   ③ postponing   ④ to postpone

09 Many products on the market are made _____ only a short time.

① to last   ② last   ③ lasted   ④ of lasting

토익 실전 문제

※ Choose the one word or phrase that best completes the sentence. (1~10)

01 The car pool program offers a more environmentally friendly way for employees
_____.

① commute   ② commutes   ③ commuted   ④ to commute

02 We keep _____documents related to criminal backgrounds in a secure file
cabinet.

① authentic   ② surrounding   ③ confidential   ④ limiting

03 Vehicles that are too wide _____through the tunnel should follow the detour
signs.

① to pass   ② pass   ③ passing   ④ are passing

04 _____cooperation, the operations manager has placed employees in
diverse program teams.

① Encouragement   ② To encourage   ③ To be encouraged   ④ Encouraged

05 Stellar Electronics is _____to have recruited innovator Zach Chambers to
lead its product development team.

① fortunate   ② promising   ③ talented   ④ obvious

06 In an effort _____the conference registration process, event organizers will
allow online registration.

① simplify   ② to simplify   ③ simplifies   ④ simplification

07 It is necessary _____basic first aid before signing up for more aadvanced
classes.

① completion   ② to be completed   ③ completing   ④ to complete

08 According to several studies, high levels of unemployment are clear _____ of economic decline.

① indicators   ② operators   ③ contractors   ④ receptors

09 Many products on the market are made _____ only a short time.

① to last   ② last   ③ lasted   ④ of lasting

10 I was so tired that I found _____ to go any farther.

① it impossible   ② unable   ③ impossible   ④ myself impossible

[정답]

1	2	3	4	5	6	7	8	9
①	②	②	④	①	①	③	①	①

1	2	3	4	5	6	7	8	9	10
④	③	①	②	①	②	④	①	①	①

 **동명사**

(1) 동명사 용법: 문장에서 주어, 보어, 목적어(전치사의 목적어)로 쓰인다.

  (ex) ① Parking here is not permitted.

     ② Seeing is believing. I'm proud of being a Korean.

     ③ I stopped smoking yesterday. (enjoy, finish, mind, avoid, consider, suggest)

      ☞ 부정사, 동명사 둘 다 목적어로 취하는 동사 → like, start, begin, love

       *위의 4 단어를 쉽게 외우는 방법 : 좋아하기 시작하면 사랑하게 된다.

(2) 동명사의 의미상의 주어

  ① 사람이나 대명사인 경우 소유격으로 한다.

   (ex) I didn't approve of John's going to a movie with us.

     Do you mind my smoking?

  ② 사물인 경우 그대로 사용한다.

   (ex) I was glad of the exam being over.

(3) 동명사의 시제

  ① 단순 동명사 (V + ing): 주절의 시제와 동일

  ② 완료 동명사 (having + p.p): 주절의 시제보다 한 시제 앞선 시제

   (ex) He regretted having done so. (=He regretted that he had done so.)

(4) 부정사와 동명사를 사용할 때의 의미차이

forget, regret remember	목적어가 부정사(미래 사실)	I forget to post the letter tomorrow.
	목적어가 동명사(과거 사실)	I forget attending the meeting then.
stop	목적어가 부정사(목적)	He stopped to smoke.
	목적어가 동명사(목적어)	You should stop smoking for your health.
try	목적어가 부정사(애쓰다)	He tried to swim across the river.
	목적어가 동명사 (시험삼아 ~해보다)	He had better try using a different graphics program.

(5) 동명사의 관용적인 표현

(ex) ① He *had difficulty* (in) solving the problem.

　　　(~하는데 어려움이 있다)

② He *is busy* (in) preparing for the exam.

　　(~하느라 바쁘다)

③ I *am used to* standing for a long time.

　　(=*be accustomed to* ~에 익숙하다)

④ He *looks forward to* meeting you again.

　　(~를 간절히 기다리다)

⑤ I *cannot help* laughing at him.

　　(~하지 않을 수 없다)

⑥ *It is no use* crying over spilt milk.

　　(~해도 소용없다)

⑦ *There is no* denying the fact.

　　(~은 불가능하다)

⑧ I don't *object to* living in the country.

　　(~에 반대하다)

⑨ Businessmen advertize to make us *feel like* buying what they sell.

　　(~하고 싶은 생각이 나다)

(6) 동명사 (부정사)의 부정: 부정어를 동명사(부정사) 앞에 둔다.

토익 기본 문제

※ Choose the best form of the underlined parts. (1~9)

01 Remember _____ the windows when you go out.

① to close   ② closing   ③ closed   ④ as closing

02 We are looking forward _____ you again.

① have seen   ② to see   ③ are seeing   ④ to seeing

03 He was arrested for _____ the car.

① the stealing   ② to steal   ③ steal   ④ stealing

04 She _____ typing the report in the morning.

① wanted   ② finished   ③ helped   ④ worried

05 The teacher told me that Francis had always enjoyed _____ English.

① studying   ② the study   ③ to study   ④ for study

06 I insisted on _____ this small present as a token of my appreciation.

① you to accept   ② your accepting   ③ your acception   ④ you accept

07 He is busy _____ a company in these days.

① to run   ② with running   ③ in running   ④ about running

08 I definitely regret _____ the letter yesterday.

① posting   ② posted   ③ to post   ④ being posted

09 It is no use _____ this discussion.

① to continuing   ② to continue   ③ of continuing   ④ continuing

토익 실전 문제

※ Choose the best form of the underlined parts. (1~10)

01 Mr. Rooney was given the responsibility of _____ an ideal venue for the company.

① find ② to find ③ finding ④ found

02 As a travel agent, Thomas Wilkinson's job is _____ the itinerary to check for scheduling programs.

① to reviewing ② reviewing ③ reviewed ④ review

03 The agency publishes a weekly magazine dedicated to _____ new technologies in the electronics field.

① highlight ② highlighting ③ highlighted ④ being highlighted

04 The vice mayor of Fresno, Joe Soprano, is an _____ of changing the current policy on the minimum.

① operator ② instructor ③ advocate ④ associate

05 An inspection by a safety officer is crucial _____ officially opening the manufacturing plant.

① yet ② some ③ only ④ before

06 _____ to articles contributed by readers are handled by the science journal's chief   editor, Mr. Kang.

① Corrections ② Correct ③ Correcting ④ Corrected

07 In order to conduct further clinical trials on the drug, we recommend _____ the deadline by one month.

① to extend   ② extension   ③ extending   ④ being extended

08 Despite _____positive feedback about the product, Mr. Lee suggested changing its design.

① having received   ② received   ③ be receiving   ④ has received

09 Would you mind _____the paper there?

① to hand to me   ② hand me   ③ handing me   ④ to handing me

10 You cannot be too careful in _____your friends.

① have chosen   ② being chosen   ③ to choose   ④ choosing

[정답]

1	2	3	4	5	6	7	8	9
①	④	④	②	①	②	③	①	④

1	2	3	4	5	6	7	8	9	10
③	②	②	③	④	①	③	①	③	④

분사

(1) 분사의 용법: 명사를 수식하거나 보어로 쓰인다.

    a) 현재분사: 능동과 진행의 의미가 강함.(진행형에 사용)

    (ex) That is an exciting game. The girl talking with Fred is Nancy.

    b) 과거분사: 수동과 완료의 의미가 강함.(완료시제에 사용)

    (ex) Put away that broken cup.

        He climbed the mountain covered with deep snow.

(2) 일반원리(예외도 있음)

	현재분사	과거분사
명사수식	명사가 생물(사람)일 때	명사가 사물일 때
주격보어	주어가 생물(사람)일 때	주어가 사물일 때
목적격보어	목적어가 생물(사람)일 때	목적어가 사물일 때

(3) 감정 동사의 분사 용법: (2)의 원리와 반대

용 법	사람이 주어인 문장 : 과거분사 사물이 주어인 문장 : 현재분사 사람을 수식하는 경우 : 과거분사 사물을 수식하는 경우 : 현재분사
감정 동사 (13개)	excite, bore, exhaust, surprise, disappoint, satisfy, interest confuse (=embarrass), please (=delight, amuse), impress

(ex) I was *bored* with listening to his *boring* address.

(4) 분사 구문: 복문을 더 간단하게 만들기 위한 방법

    먼저, 접속사를 없애고 둘째, 부사절의 주어가 주절의 주어와 같으면 생략하고 (다를 경우는 그대로 둠), 마지막으로 부사절 동사를 현재분사로 바꾼다.

    (ex) ① Walking along the street, I met a friend of mine.

        (=While I was walking along the street, I met a friend of mine.)

② Having nothing to do, I went to bed earlier.

(=Because I had nothing to do, I went to bed earlier.)

③ Being young, she has much experience.

(=Though she is young, she has much experience.)

(5) 계속적 용법: and V

(ex) I hurried to the station, *catching the express train in time.*

(=and caught the express train in time.)

(6) 분사구문의 부정: 부정어를 분사 구문 앞에 둔다.

(ex) Not knowing what to do, I asked for his advice.

(7) 관용 표현: Generally speaking ~, Frankly speaking ~

(ex) Frankly speaking, this is not true.

(8) 독립 분사 구문: 주절과 종속절의 주어가 다른 경우는 현재분사 앞에 그대로 쓴다.

(ex) It being fine, we went out for a walk.

(9) 부대상황: with+ 목적어+ 분사 (~하면서, ~한 채로)

(ex) He sleeps with his mouth open.

(with my mouth full/ with your eyes shut)

토익 기본 문제

※ Choose the best form of the underlined parts. (1~9)

01 State laws can't conflict with those _____ by the federal government.

① passing   ② passed   ③ to pass   ④ pass

02 He spoke for a long time and his speech was very _____.

① boring   ② bored   ③ bore   ④ boredom

03 _____ found, four-leaf clover is considered as a lucky sign.

① It is rarely   ② Rarely   ③ The rare   ④ Being rarely

04 Do you know the boy _____ over there?

① stood   ② that stand   ③ standing   ④ to have stood

05 He got his bag _____ in the train doors as they were closed.

① to be caught   ② catch   ③ catching   ④ caught

06 I heard my name _____ by my teacher.

① call   ② calling   ③ called   ④ to call

07 The girl _____ with Tom is Rosa.

① talking   ② talked   ③ is talking   ④ is talked

08 He climbed the mountain _____ with deep snow.

① to cover   ② that covers   ③ is covered   ④ covered

09 Not _____ healthy, he always stays home.

① because he was   ② being   ③ to be   ④ because he is

토익 실전 문제

※ Choose the best form of the underlined parts. (1~10)

01 The enclosed pamphlet contains comprehensive details about your recently _____ bank loan.

① issued   ② issue   ③ being issued   ④ issuing

02 Ms. Boothroyd has made several _____ decisions to boost sales in North American markets.

① contented   ② unanimous   ③ strategic   ④ reflected

03 Big River Magine is providing an _____ deadline to contest participants who couldn't upload photos due to the Web site malfunction.

① extensive   ② extended   ③ extend   ④ extends

04 Ms. Arnett was _____ by the lack of features on the digital camera, considering the price that she paid.

① disappointed   ② disappointedly   ③ disappointing   ④ to disappoint

05 By following the guidelines _____ in the user manual, you can prolong the life of the product.

① outlining   ② outlined   ③ outline   ④ outlines

06 It is Mr. Harrison's responsibility to provide shareholders with timely _____ of monthly overseas sales.

① finances   ② estimates   ③ features   ④ deposits

07 Staff members are reminded to turn off the air conditioning when _____ the meeting room.

① exit   ② exited   ③ exits   ④ exiting

08 Many of the world's most _____ musicians will be in attendance at 13th Annual Montreal Jazz Festival.

① rewarding   ② accomplished   ③ complicated   ④ remaining

09 It was a really _____ experience. Afterwards everybody was extremely.

① terrifying, shocked   ② terrifying, shocking
③ terrified, shocked   ④ terrified, shocking

10 Mr. Park sometimes feels _____ because his English is not very good.

① disappointed   ② to be disappointed   ③ disappoint   ④ disappointing

[정답]

1	2	3	4	5	6	7	8	9
②	①	②	③	④	③	①	④	②

1	2	3	4	5	6	7	8	9	10
①	③	②	①	②	②	④	②	①	①

접속사 (전치사)

(1) 등위 접속사: 문법적으로 같은 역할을 하는 단어, 구, 그리고 절을 연결한다.

☞ **병렬구조:** 등위접속사, 상관접속사에 의해 단어, 구, 절이 연결될 경우에는 동일한 형태가 나와야 한다.

(ex) ① He improves in his English slowly *but* steadily.

② That house is to let *or* to sell

③ Would you prefer coffee *or* tea?

④ They worked *both* by day *and* by night.

⑤ He must *either* call his father *or* write to him.

⑥ *Not only* does he drive his car, *but* he *also* repairs it for himself.

(2) 종속 접속사: 명사절, 형용사절, 부사절이 있다.

① 명사절: 문장에서 주어, 목적어, 보어로 쓰이는 that, 그리고 간접의문문에 쓰이는 의문사가 있다.

(ex) That he will come is certain. (=It is certain that he will come.)

　　　I know that he works hard.

② 형용사절: 관계사절

③ 부사절: 시간, 장소, 이유, 양보 그리고 목적(결과)을 나타내는 문장을 이끈다.

용법	접속사 종류	예 문
때	when, as, while, before, as soon as, after	When I was a child, I was sick. While there is life, there is hope.
조건	if, unless	If you turn to the left, you will find the bank.
이유	as, because, for, now that, since	Because she is near-sighted, she always wears glasses. He felt no fear, for he was a brave man.
양보	though, although even if, even though	Although they are poor, they are happy. (=In spite of their poverty, they are happy.)
목적	so that~may(can)	He goes there (so) that he may meet him.
결과	so~that	It was so hot that we went swimming.

☞ 종속접속사와 전치사구의 차이점

종속접속사는 절을 이끌지만, 전치사구는 전치사 다음에 반드시 명사(상당어구)가 온다.

	종속 접속사	전치사(구)
시 간	when, while	during, for
이 유	because, as, since	because of, owing to
양 보	although, (even) though	despite, in spite of
조 건	unless	without

토익 기본 문제

※ Choose the best form of the underlined parts. (1~9)

01 Chemistry is the science of substances _____ the science of energy.

① is physics   ② or physics   ④ how physics   ④ and physics is

02 We have many rivals not only in Korea _____ in the United States.

① as well as   ② but also   ③ and   ④ or

03 All products can be classified as either consumer goods _____ producer goods.

① for   ② by   ③ so   ④ or

04 _____ large in volume, a comet is small in mass.

① It is   ② How it is   ③ Although it is   ④ When is it

05 Mr. Scott skipped because _____ so many reports to write.

① there were   ② there was   ③ he can have   ④ could have

06 Children were evacuated to the country _____ the war.

① while   ② when   ③ during   ④ where

07 The thief entered her room slowly and _____.

① silent   ② silence   ③ silently   ④ very silent

08 Both the TV ads _____ the newspaper ads will be withdrawn.

① also   ② but also   ③ nor   ④ and

09 It was so hot _____ swimming.

① that he went   ② as it was   ③ that went   ④ how to

토익 실전 문제

※ Choose the best form of the underlined parts. (1~10)

01 _____ Mr. Saito departed for the airport, he had printed a copy of his itinerary.

① Before   ② Until   ③ Unless   ④ Through

02 Ms. Everton spent morning months trying to find an effective _____ for her medical condition.

① involvement   ② treatment   ③ injury   ④ origin

03 Visitors must pay for the museum's special exhibition, _____ they can browse the permanent collection for free.

① so that   ② despite   ③ because   ④ although

04 The manager's concern is _____ several employees in her division have called in sick this morning.

① as   ② that   ③ while   ④ whether

05 _____ the director approves the proposal from the security department, employees will be issued electronic key cards.

① Provide   ② Provides   ③ Provided   ④ Provision

06 Ms. Evans _____ that nominations for the Employee of the Month Award were being accepted vie e-mail.

① happened   ② displayed   ③ requested   ④ announced

07 Ms. Grey does not know _____ management has decided to sell off the subsidiary.

① for   ② as   ③ if   ④ because

08 Most merchandise can be returned within thirty days of purchase _____it was a custom order

① in case   ② unless   ③ instead   ④ during

09 When they were written, many nursery rhymes were intended not for children _____for adults.

① nevertheless   ② but
③ instead of   ④ on the other hand

10 Staff members are being asked to postpone any vacations _____ the entire project has been completed.

① during   ② until   ③ because   ④ since

[정답]

1	2	3	4	5	6	7	8	9
④	②	④	③	①	③	③	④	①

1	2	3	4	5	6	7	8	9	10
①	②	④	②	③	④	③	②	②	②

관계절

(1) 관계대명사: 복문에서 주절과 관계대명사절을 연결하는 <u>접속사+대명사</u> 역할을 하는 단어로서, 바로 앞에 나온 선행사를 수식한다.

(ex) I know a child. + She is always biting her nails.

(=I know the child who is always biting her nails.)

여기에서 who=and she, the child는 선행사이다.

(2) 관계대명사 종류

선행사의 종류	주 격	소 유 격	목 적 격
사람	who	whose	whom
사물, 동물	which	whose, of which	which
사람, 동물, 사물	that	없음	that
선행사 포함	what	없음	what

① **which**: 선행사가 동물이거나 사물일 때 사용하며, 계속적 용법에서 선행사가 구 (phrase)나 절(sentence)일 때도 쓰인다.

(ex) The Thames is the river which flows through London.

He divorced his wife, which surprised me.

② **that**: who, which 대신에 사용되며, [전치사+that]나 계속적 용법에는 사용하지 않는다.

(단, all, everything, the only 그리고 최상급 다음에는 주로 that를 쓰는 경향이 있다.)

(ex) ⓐ *All* that glitters is not gold.

ⓑ This is *the best* hotel (that) I know. (최상급이 선행사)

ⓒ She has written about *the people and things* that interest her.

(사람과 사물이 선행사)

ⓓ *Who* that has common sense can say such a thing?(의문사가 선행사)

ⓔ He is *the only* man that I can trust.

③ **what**: 선행사가 포함된 관계대명사를 말한다. (=the thing(s) that)

(ex) What we saw astonished us.

(=The things that we saw astonished us.)

(3) 관계대명사의 생략: 제한적 용법에서 목적격은 생략가능하며, [전치사+관계대명사]인 경우 관계대명사가 생략되면 전치사는 문장 끝으로 이동한다.

(ex) This is the best hotel (that) I know.

John likes the house he lives in.

(4) 관계부사: 관계부사는 where, when, how, why가 있으며, 접속사+부사 역할을 한다. 따라서, 관계부사절 다음에는 완전한 문장이 온다.

☞ ① 관계 부사는 선행사가 명사일 경우 전치사+which로 바꿀 수 있다.

(ex) This is the place where(=in which) he was born.

② 관계 부사는 where를 제외하고 생략이 가능하다.

(ex) This is the reason (why) I stopped smoking.

③ 관계 부사 where, when은 계속적 용법으로 쓰일 수 있다.

(ex) In 1939, when World War Ⅱ broke out, my father was born in Paris.

관계대명사와 관계부사 그리고 접속사(that)의 구별방법
① 관계대명사 다음에는 불완전한 문장 (주어나 목적어가 없는)이 온다.
② 관계 부사 다음에는 완전한 문장이 나온다.
③ 접속사(that) 다음에는 완전한 문장이 나온다.
(차이 : 명사 + 관계부사 / 타동사 + 접속사 that)

---

(5) 유사관계대명사: 본래는 관계대명사가 아니지만 가끔 관계대명사의 역할을 하는 as, but, than을 말한다.

(ex) 1. As many students as attended the meeting were given presents.

2. What's the same problem as bothers you?

3. There is no rule but has some exceptions.

4. Don't use more words than are necessary.

토익 기본 문제

※ Choose the best form of the underlined parts. (1~9)

01 He bought the boat _____ at the boat show.

① saw it　② that he saw　③ that he saw it　④ it that he saw

02 _____ you say may be true.

① That　② Which　③ What　④ Whose

03 Professor Park lives in a city in _____ a car is almost a necessity.

① whose　② where　③ what　④ which

04 The boy _____ I believed to be honest deceived me.

① whose　② what　③ which　④ whom

05 John was the only one _____ I had invited.

① which　② that　③ whom　④ who

06 The man _____ hat blew off in the wind chased it across the park.

① his　② whose　③ who　④ that

07 He arrived half an hour late, _____ annoyed us very much.

① that　② as　③ which　④ what

08 The year _____ I was born was very eventful.

① why　② which　③ where　④ when

09 I saw a man _____ I thought of a friend of his.

① who　② whom　③ which　④ to whom

토익 실전 문제

※ Choose the best form of the underlined parts. (1~10)

01 Attendees _____purchase conference tickets in advance will be guaranteed premium seating.

① who   ② themselves   ③ whose   ④ they

02 The regional manager will explain the details of the _____relocation to Fraize Lake.

① numerous   ② upcoming   ③ adjacent   ④ frequent

03 Hikers can get information about native plants from the brochure that ____the trail map.

① accompaniment   ② accompanies   ③ accompanying   ④ accompany

04 Seaside Restaurant, _____chef underwent intensive training in Italy, received positive reviews from food critics.

① which   ② who   ③ whatever   ④ whose

05 The detergent should not be used by _____who are allergic to certain chemicals.

① materials   ② locations   ③ individuals   ④ directions

06 Please _____your appointment with Mr. Walsh by calling his assistant no later than June 12.

① confirm   ② remind   ③ agree   ④ comply

07 The poor business model is _____caused the software developer to go bankrupt.

① whose   ② who   ③ what   ④ which

08 The admission ticket shows the time _____the performance begins.

① which   ② how   ③ when   ④ why

09 I will employ the man _____they say is a fluent speaker of English.

① who   ② whom   ③ what   ④ where

10 She is one of the most beautiful girls _____I have ever met.

① that   ② which   ③ whom   ④ what

[정답]

1	2	3	4	5	6	7	8	9
②	③	④	④	②	②	③	④	②

1	2	3	4	5	6	7	8	9	10
①	②	②	④	③	①	③	③	①	①

 **가정법**

(1) 가정법 종류 및 형태

종 류	형태 및 의미(예문)
가정법 현재	현재, 또는 미래에 대한 불확실한 (확률은 50~60%) 상황을 가정한다. If+S+V(현재형)~, S+조동사 현재(will, shall, can, may)+V(원형) (ex) If he confesses, I shall overlook the offence.
가정법 과거	현재 사실에 반대되는 것을 가정한다. If+S+V(과거형)~, S+조동사 과거(would, should, could, might)+V (ex) If I were rich, I could buy the car. 　　(=Because I am not rich, I can't buy the car.)
가정법 과거완료	과거 사실에 반대되는 것을 가정한다. If+S+V(과거완료 :had+p.p), S+조동사과거(would, should, could, might)+have+p.p (ex) If he had had money, he could have bought a new car. 　　(=Because he didn't have money, he couldn't buy a new car.)
가정법 미래	현재, 또는 미래에서 가능성이 희박한 경우에 사용한다. If+S+[should, were to]+V(원형), S+조동사 현재 혹은 과거+V(원형) (ex) If it should rain, I would take you home by car. 　　(확률은 80~90% 불가능) (ex) If the sun were to rise in the west, I would change my 　　mind.(확률은 100% 불가능)

(2) wish 용법: that+가정법 과거 : 현재 사실의 반대를 소망

　　　　　　　that+가정법 과거완료 : 과거 사실의 반대를 소망

　(ex) I wish that the rain stopped.

　　　(=I am sorry the rain doesn't stop.)

　　　I wish he had been here yesterday.

　　　(=I am sorry he wasn't here yesterday.)

(3) but for (=without)용법: 가정법 과거나 가정법 과거완료

　(ex) But for his advice, I would fail.

(=If it were not for his advice, I would fail.)

But for his help, I couldn't have passed the exam.

(=If it had not been for his help, I couldn't have passed the exam.)

(4) 제안, 주장, 요구를 나타내는 동사의 that절

형 식	S+동사(suggest, propose, insist, demand, require) +that+ S+(should)+동사원형
	It is 형용사(important, necessary, natural)+that+S+(should) +동사원형

(ex)   She suggested that he (should) go to Europe.

└ 동사 추가 (request, recommend)

(5) 혼합가정법: (주절과 조건절의 시제가 다른 경우)

(ex) As he helped me *then*, I am alive *now*.

(=If he had not helped me then, I should not be alive now.)

(6) If 생략: 조건절의 if 생략

(ex) 1. Were I you, I could buy it. (=If I were you, I could buy it.)

2. Had he not been ill, he would have gone there.

(= If he had not been ill, he would have gone there.)

3. Should it rain, I would take you home by car.

(=If it should rain, I would take you home by car.)

토익 기본 문제

※ Choose the best form of the underlined parts. (1~9)

01 If you _____ a million dollars, what would you do?

① have   ② would have   ③ had   ④ have had

02 If it _____ on Friday, we'll definitely have to go skiing.

① snow   ② snows   ③ will snow   ④ snowed

03 If I had had more time in Paris, I _____ seen a few more cathedrals.

① can   ② will   ③ would   ④ would have

04 If I had not missed the plane, I _____ have arrived so late.

① will   ② won't   ③ would   ④ wouldn't

05 The hostess insisted that we _____ the soup.

① testing   ② to taste   ③ tasted   ④ taste

06 _____ the money he lent me, I couldn't have bought a new car.

① With   ② Though   ③ Because of   ④ But for

07 If I _____ a mayor, I would make the streets cleaner and hire more policemen.

① am   ② were   ③ would be   ④ be

08 If the sun _____ in the west, I would not do so.

① will rise   ② rises   ③ were to rise   ④ rise

09 If it were not ___ his advice, I would fail.

① for   ② to   ③ except   ④ with

토익 실전 문제

※ Choose the best form of the underlined parts. (1~10)

01 If I saw the damage to your house, I _____you an estimate for the repair costs.

① could give   ② have given   ③ gave   ④ give

02 Spa patrons should indicate their music _____before going into the massage.

① discretion   ② advantage   ③ recognition   ④ preference

03 If the promotional displays _____in a more visible spot, a greater number of customers would have purchased the products.

① placed   ② had been placed   ③ place   ④ are placed

04 If the sales representative had not apologized for his actions, I would _____a formal complaint with the general manager.

① be filed   ② had filed   ③ have filed   ④ been filed

05 To _____a private conference room, please submit an official requet to Mr. Baldwin.

① direct   ② decide   ③ reserve   ④ stand

06 Young's Carpeting could begin laying the office carpets today _____the painting were completed.

① even   ② both   ③ if   ④ or

07 Mr. Burnage may contact some successful local business owners _____extra funding be required to start his new restaurant.

① when   ② should   ③ in fact   ④ through

08 Were there a better selection of clothing, we _____ at this store more often.

① would stop   ② shopped   ③ are shopping   ④ were shopping

09 If we had not developed pur own recreation program then, we _____ nothing to do for fun now.

① have   ② had   ③ would have   ④ would have been

10 Without oxygen, all animals _____ long ago.

① would have disappeared   ② would disappear

③ would be disappeared   ④ had disappeared

[정답]

1	2	3	4	5	6	7	8	9
③	②	④	④	④	④	②	③	①

1	2	3	4	5	6	7	8	9	10
①	④	②	③	③	③	②	①	③	①

Part 2 ... 토익 어휘

◎ 신 토익 어휘 출제 경향

1. part 5: 어휘 출제 경향과 전략 (어휘 출제 수: 평균 14~16 문제)

'어휘 문제는 해석 문제이다.' 라고 오해하는 경우가 많다. 어휘 14~16문제 중 과연 해석을 통해 풀어야 하는 문제가 얼마나 될까? 2~3문제를 제외하고는 거의 없다. 신토익에서 출제되는 문제를 보면, 동사 'obey'는 '따르다, 복종하다' 의 의미로 목적어로 반드시 'law, rule, order' 등이 연결되어 같이 나온다. 명사 'increase' 는 뒤에 반드시 전치사 'in'이 나오는 표현이다. 따라서 어휘를 어휘로 암기하는 것보다 단짝 표현 중심으로 암기하면 빨리 풀 수 있다.

2. part 6: 어휘 출제 경향과 전략 (어휘 출제 수: 평균 7~8 문제)

part 6는 파트 5와 part 7의 경계선에 준지문의 성격을 띠고 있다. 따라서 1차적으로 빈칸이 속한 문장과 그 주변 문장의 도움을 받아야한다. 즉 문장의 문맥을 이용해서 예측해야 하는 것이다. 또한 빈칸 채워 넣기 문제를 제외하고 거의 매회 출제되는 문제들이 있는데, 시제, 접속부사, 반의어 등은 유념해서 보아야 한다. 특히 4개의 선택지 중 반대의 뜻을 가진 어휘가 있다면 둘 중 하나를 선택하는 문제로 봐야 한다.

3. part 7: 어휘 출제 경향과 전략 (동의어 출제 수: 평균 1~3 문제)

part 7 어휘 문제는 통상 동의어 문제라고 하지만, 실은 문맥상 잘 어울리는 어휘 즉 대체 어휘를 찾는 문제이다. 동의어 문제라면 제시된 단어와 같은 의미를 가진 단어를 선택지에서 찾으면 된다. 하지만 실제로 비슷한 의미를 지닌 여러 단어들이 동시에 선택지에 제시되는 경우가 있다. 이럴 때는 반드시 주어진 단어가 문장에서 어떤 의미로 사용되었는지를 파악한 후 대신 할 수 있는 단어를 선택지에서 찾는 식으로 해결해야 한다.

토익 기본 단어

tradition   전통, 전설
share   몫, 할당, 분배하다, 공유하다
obscure   애매한, 모호한
hideous   무서운, 끔찍한, 불쾌한
combination   결합, 배합, 조합
coincide   동시에 일어나다
competition   경쟁, 시합
fierce   사나운, 맹렬한
retreat   물러서다, 퇴각, 후퇴
enemy   적, 적수, 적국의, 적의
supply   공급하다, 배달하다
accuse   고발하다, 비난하다
drug   약, 제약, 마약
arrest   체포하다, 체포, 검거
charge   책임, 비난, (요금을) 청구하다
murder   살인, 살인 사건, 살해하다
commit   (죄 등을) 범하다
crime   죄, 범죄
constitute   구성하다, 제정하다
stable   안정적인
circumstance   환경, 사정, 상황
constant   불변의, 끊임없는, 견실한
distant   먼, 멀리 있는
substance   물체, 본질, 실체
pollution   오염
author   저자, 작가

guilty   유죄의, (과실 등을) 저지른
innocent   무죄의, 순진한, 순결한
injure   상처를 입히다, 해를 주다
explosion   폭발, 파열
bomb   폭탄, 폭격하다
parachute   낙하산, 낙하산을 타다
confiscate   압수하다, 몰수하다
provide   공급하다, 주다, 준비하다
solution   해결, 용해, 녹임
violence   폭력, 격렬함, 폭행
patrol   순찰, 정찰, 순찰병, 순찰하다
riot   폭동, 소요, 폭동을 일으키다
block   막다, 봉쇄하다, 건물 한 구획
convict   유죄를 입증(선고)하다
robbery   강도, 도둑질, 강탈
institution   학원, 협회, 제도, 설립
destitute   결핍한, 빈곤한, 가난한
prostitute   매춘하다, 매음하다
substitute   대신하다, 대리하다
superstition   미신, 미신적 습관
ladder   사닥다리
estate   재산, 자산, 부동산, 소유지
recognize   알아차리다, 깨닫다
immediately   곧, 즉시
affect   ~에 영향을 미치다
symptom   증상, 징후

transcribe 옮겨 쓰다, 베끼다

describe 묘사하다

subscriber 서명자, 기부자, 찬성자

major 주요한, 대다수의

vivid 생생한, 발랄한, 생기 있는

scenery 풍경, 경치, 배경

increase 증가하다, 늘다, 늘리다

launch (배를) 진수시키다, 착수하다

submarine 잠수함, 해저의

marine 해양의, 바다의, 해병대원

mammal 포유동물

perish 멸망하다, 죽다, 타락하다

earthquake 지진

destruction 파괴

force 힘, 억지로(강제로)시키다

reinforce 강화하다, 보강하다

weapon 무기

lethal 치명적인, 치사의, 죽음의

inject 주사하다, 주입하다, 삽입하다

execute 실행하다, 수행하다,

disappoint 실망시키다

appoint 지명하다, 임명하다

failure 실패

government 정부, 정치

inform 알리다, 통보하다

escape 달아나다, 도피하다, 탈출

serious 진지한, 중대한, 심각한

bruise 멍, 타박상

electric 전기의, 전기 장치의

amazing 놀랄 만한, 굉장한

cease 그치다, 끝내다, 그만두다

remind 생각나게 하다, 상기시키다

assemble 모으다, 집합시키다

emergency 비상사태, 긴급한

disabled 불구가 된, 무능력해진

mentally 정신적으로

physical 물질적인, 육체의

blow (바람이) 불다, 강타, 강풍

tidy 단정한, 말쑥한, 깔끔한

neat 산뜻한, 말쑥한

stitch 한 바늘, 한 땀, 꿰매다

scar 상처, 흉터, 상처를 남기다

psychology 심리학

refugee 피난민, 망명자, 도망자

border 국경, 경계, 가장자리

flee 달아나다, 도망치다

capture 사로잡다, 포획하다

battle 전투, 싸움

rebel 반역자, 반역의, 반역하다

cause 원인, 이유

root 뿌리, 근원

behavior 행동, 행실, 태도

threat 위협, 협박

notice 통지, 통보, 주의, 알아차리다

critical 비평적인, 비판적인, 위기의

waste 낭비하다, 낭비

dump (쓰레기를) 내버리다

material 물질, 재료, 물질적인

modernism 현대 사상

synthetic 종합의, 합성의, 인조의

postscript 추신(p.s)

prescribe (약 등을) 처방하다

disguise   변장시키다, 위장하다
shave   면도하다
beard   턱수염
false   그릇된, 거짓의, 틀린
evidence   증거
damage   손해, 손상
extent   범위, 정도, 넓이
restrict   제한하다, 금지하다
measure   측정하다, 치수, 조처
morale   사기, 의욕
enormous   거대한, 막대한, 엄청난
afford   (경제적 시간적) 여유가 있다
rent   빌다, 임차하다, 임대하다, 임대
spare   예비의, 아끼다
search   찾다, 수색하다, 수색
effort   노력, 분투
expand   팽창시키다, 팽창하다,
reduce   줄이다, 감소시키다
nuclear   핵의, 원자핵의
fog   안개
wrap   싸다, 포장하다, 싸개, 덮개
ignore   무시하다
regulate   규정하다, 조정하다
achieve   성취하다, 얻다
suitable   적당한, 어울리는, 알맞은
celebrate   축하하다, 기념하다
anniversary   기념일
revolution   혁명, 대변혁
eventually   결국, 드디어
export   수출하다, 수출
import   수입하다, 수입
transport   운송하다, 수송하다

plenty   많은, 많음
ample   많은, 풍부한
complement   보충, 보충하다
supplement   보충, 보충하다
complete   완전한, 완성하다
deplete   고갈시키다, 비우다
perfect   완벽한
resource   자원
source   근원, 원천, 출처
environment   환경, 분위기
create   창조하다, 창작하다
bottom   밑바닥, 기초
amazing   놀랄 만한, 굉장한
stare   응시하다, 바라보다, 빤히 봄
wound   상처, 상해, 상처를 입히다
horror   공포, 전율
workmate   직장동료
pour   따르다, 붓다, 퍼붓다
civil   시민의
civilization   문명, 개화
effective   효과적인, 효력 있는
radiation   복사, 방사, 방사능
disaster   재앙, 불행, 재난
warn   경고하다
global   지구의, 세계적인
goods   상품, 화물
cliff   절벽, 벼랑, 낭떠러지
edge   모서리, 가장자리, 위기
collapse   붕괴하다
support   지지하다, 부양하다
encourage   용기를 북돋우다
construct   건설하다

profitable 유리한, 이익이 되는

textile 직물, 직물의

income 수입, 소득

producer 생산자, 제작자, 연출가

industry 산업, 근면

assist 돕다, 원조하다

finance 재정, 재무

budget 예산, 운영비, 경비

committee 위원회

recycle 재활용하다

local 지방의

population 인구, 주민

popular 대중적인, 인기 있는, 민중의

prove 입증하다, ~으로 판명되다

approve 승인하다, 인정하다

climb 오르다, 기어오르다

rescue 구출하다, 구조하다, 구출

sink 가라앉다, 침몰하다

despair 절망, 자포자기

prospect 전망, 경치

perspective 전망, 가망

spectacle 광경, 구경거리

speculate 사색하다

inspect 조사하다, 시찰하다

monologue 독백

monopoly 독점, 전매

monotonous 단조로운

routine 일상의, 틀에 박힌 일, 일과

disgrace 불명예, 치욕

bear 곰, 참다, 견디다, 낳다

brutal 야만적인, 짐승의, 잔인한

respect 존경하다

suspect 의심하다, 혐의를 두다

conspicuous 눈에 잘 띄는, 현저한

perspicuous 명료한, 분명한

perspicacious 총명한, 통찰력 있는

despise 경멸하다, 멸시하다

aspect 국면, 양상, 관점

worry 걱정시키다, 걱정하다

election 선거

represent 대표하다, 나타내다

victim 희생, 희생자

rape 강간, 강탈, 강간하다

drag 끌다, 끌고 가다

argue 논쟁하다, 주장하다

exist 존재하다

persist 고집하다, 참다

resist 저항하다, 반대하다, 항거하다

subsist 존재하다, 살아가다

insist 주장하다

consist 이루어지다, 일치하다

dish 요리, 음식

vegetable 야채, 채소

prepare 준비하다, 마련하다

sewage 하수, 하수 오물

install (장비, 장치 등을) 설치하다

gravity 중력, 인력

mediate 중재하다, 조정하다

keen 날카로운, 예민한, 신랄한

face 직면하다, ~를 향하다

bother 괴롭히다

temporary 일시적인, 임시의

emotion 감정
resign   사직하다, 사임하다
culture   문화, 교양
identity   신원, 독자성, 동일성
apparent   분명한, 명백한, 외관상의
judge   재판하다, 판단하다, 판사
prejudice   선입관, 편견
aim   겨누다, 목표 삼다, 목적
compromise   타협하다, 타협
policy   정책, 방침
involve   포함하다
operate   수술하다
repair   고치다, 수선하다, 수선
delicate 섬세한, 민감한, 미묘한
ripe   익은, 숙성한
instinct   본능
produce   생산하다, 창작하다
fertile   비옥한, 다산의
desert   버리다, 저버리다, 사막
canal   운하, 수로
method   방법, 수단
privilege   특권, 특권을 주다
obtain   얻다, 획득하다
abstain   삼가다, 억제하다, 끊다
retain   보유하다, 계속 유지하다
sustain   떠받치다, 유지하다
attain   달성하다, 얻다, 성취하다
independence   독립, 자주
advertise   광고하다, 선전하다
knight   (중세의) 기사, 무사
bravery   용기, 용감

prosecute   고발하다, 기소하다,
neglect   게을리 하다, 태만
infancy   유년, 초기
recently   최근에, 요즘에
mortal   죽어야할 운명의, 치명적인
decrease   줄다, 감소하다, 줄이다
steady   확고한, 안정된, 한결같은
progressive 진보적인, 혁신적인
annoy   괴롭히다, 성가시게 굴다
treatment   처리, 대우, 치료법
fury   격노, 격분
medicine 약, 의학, 내과
medical   의학의, 의약의
symptom   증상, 징후
temperature   기온, 온도
complain   불평하다
offence   공격, 위반, 반칙
corrupt   타락한, 부정한
interrupt   (대화 등을) 방해하다
bankrupt 파산한, 파산시키다
erupt   (화산이) 분출하다, 폭발하다
diplomacy   외교, 외교술
disappear   사라지다
regime   정권, 제도, 통치권
preside   사회하다, 주재하다
reside   살다, 거주하다
consider 숙고하다, 고려하다
colleague (주로 관직, 교수, 공무 등 직업상의) 동료
entertain 즐겁게 하다, 대접하다, 환대하다

impulse　충동, 원동력

virtue　미덕, 덕행, 선, 장점

patience　인내, 참을성

sigh　한숨 쉬다, 한숨

attack　공격, 공격하다, 폭행하다

defeat　쳐부수다, 패배시키다

ambition　야망, 큰 뜻

ultimate　궁극적인, 최후의

conflict　투쟁, 투쟁하다, 싸우다

aggress　공격하다, 시비를 걸다

responsibility　책임, 의무

terrible　무시무시한, 대단한, 엄청난

situation　위치, 상황, 사태

organization　조직, 단체

stimulus　자극

attempt　시도하다, 시도

tempt　유혹하다, 꾀다, 부추기다

admonish　혼내다, 훈계하다, 꾸짖다

vanity　허영심, 허무함

mirror　거울, 반사경

reflect　반사하다, 숙고하다

surface　표면, 외면

liberty　자유, 해방

emphasize　강조하다

conform　따르다, 순응하다

extinguish　(불, 빛 등을) 끄다

flame　불꽃, 화염

brilliant　빛나는, 찬란한, 훌륭한

evolve　진화하다, 발전하다

research　(학술) 연구, 조사

suggest　제안하다, 암시하다,

disturb　방해하다

domestic　가정의, 국내의

chore　(가정의) 허드렛일

feed　먹이를 주다,

save　(사람을) 구하다, 저축하다

artificial　인조의, 인공의, 가짜의

surgeon　외과 의사

jealous　질투심 많은, 시기하는

fatigue　피로, 지치게 하다

suffer　고생하다, 괴로워하다

relate　관계시키다, 말하다

spoil　망치다, (성격 등을) 버리다

rude　버릇없는, 무례한

compassion　연민, 공감

pathetic　감상적인, 애처로운

antipathy　반감, 혐오

sympathy　동정, 공감

apathy　무감각, 무관심, 냉담

passion　열정

extraordinary　이상한, 보통이 아닌,

색indicate　나타내다, 가리키다

envious　시기심이 강한, 부러워하는

fair　공평한, 공정한

shatter　산산이 부수다

illusion　환영, 망상

hypocrisy　위선

pretend　~인 체하다, 가장하다

neutral　중립의, 중립국의, 중성의

enhance　(질, 능력 등을) 높이다

contain　포함하다

maintain　유지하다, 주장하다

ordinary 보통의, 평범한

distinguish 구별하다

detail 세부 사항, 상세히 말하다

correct 정정하다, 바로잡다, 올바른

erect 직립의, 똑바로 선

rectangle 직사각형, 장방형

direct 지시하다, 관리하다, 직접적인

negotiate 협상하다, 교섭하다

deny 부인하다

illegal 불법적인

press 내리 누르다, 압박하다, 신문

pressure 압력

compress 압축하다

depress 의기소침하게 하다

express 표현하다, 발표하다

oppress 압박하다, 억압하다

suppress 억압하다, 진압하다

rage 격노, 분노, 격노하다, 날뛰다

outrage 난폭, 폭행, 격분시키다

parliament 의회

assassination 암살

security 안전, 보증

investment 투자

efficient 효과 있는, 능률적인

improve 개선하다, 진보시키다

calamity 재난, 불행

ruin 파멸시키다, 망치다, 파멸

previous 이전의, 앞의

abroad 해외에, 해외로, 널리

individual 개인의, 개개의, 개인

preserve 보존하다, 보호하다

impression 인상, 감명

repute 평판

acquire 얻다, 획득하다

inquire 묻다, 질문하다

request 요청, 요구, 요구하다

require 요구하다, 필요로 하다

conquer 정복하다, 공략하다

prefer 오히려 ~을 더 좋아하다

avoid 피하다, 회피하다

latest 최신의, 최근의, 가장 늦은

divorce 이혼시키다, 이혼

lament 슬퍼하다, 애도하다, 비탄

decline 기울다, 쇠퇴하다, 쇠퇴

influence 영향, 영향을 미치다

influenza 독감(= flu)

superfluous 여분의, 남아도는

fluent 유창한

vital 생명의, 치명적인, 극히 중대한

urgent 긴급한, 절박한

endeavor 노력, 노력하다

positive 적극적인, 확신하는

attitude 태도, 자세

adopt 채택(채용)하다, 받아들이다,
　　　　양자(양녀)로 삼다

formation 형성, 편성, 대형, 편대

formation 형성, 편성, 대형, 편대

barely 거의 ~않다, 간신히, 겨우

bare 발가벗은, 노출된

advance 진전하다, 전진하다, 전진
　　　　시키다, 앞서의, 사전의

tact 재치, 요령

indispensable 필요 불가결한

acknowledge 인정하다, 승인하다

precious 귀중한, 값비싼

property 재산, 소유권

privacy 사생활, 사적인 생활

protect 보호하다, 비호하다

function 기능, 역할, 기능을 하다

vein 정맥, 혈관

artery 동맥

distribute 분배하다, 배분하다

attribute ~탓으로 돌리다, 속성

contribute 공헌하다, 기부하다

enthusiasm 열광, 열의, 열중

delay 연장하다, 늦추다, 연기

persuade 설득하다

final 마지막의

infinite 무한한, 끝없는

finale 끝, 대단원, 피날레

definite 한정된, 명확한

confine 한정하다, 제한하다

exquisite 정교한, 절묘한, 우아한

vessel (큰) 배, 그릇

refuge 피난, 피난처

seek 찾다, 추구하다

persecution 박해

hazard 위험

accept 받아들이다, 수락하다

occupation 직업, 업무

hesitation 주저, 망설임

nervous 신경(성)의, 신경과민의

expert 전문가, 숙련가, 숙련된

significant 중요한, 의미 있는

tropic 열대지방

retire 은퇴하다, 퇴직하다

volunteer 지원자, 자진하여 하다

literal 글자 그대로의

literary 문학의

merit 장점, 공로

sufficient 충분한

deficient 부족한, 불충분한

insure 보증하다, 보험에 들다

certify 증명하다, 보증하다

insane 제정신이 아닌, 미친

zealous 열광적인, 열심인, 열중인

ban 금지령, 금지, 금지하다

treaty 조약, 협정

currency 통화, 유통

union 연합, 동맹, 화합, 연합의

unify 통합하다

unity 통일, 조화, 단일(성)

unanimity 만장일치, 동의

universe 우주

unique 유일한, 독특한

fossil 화석, 화석의

skeleton 해골, 뼈대

explorer 탐험가

planet 행성, 유성

vital 생명의, 극히 중대한

oppose 반대하다, 대항하다

democracy 민주정치, 민주주의

epidemic 유행성의, 전염성의

demonstrate 데모하다, 증명하다

settle 자리 잡다, 정착하다, 해결하다

claim 요구하다, 청구하다, 주장하다

stir 휘젓다, 흔들다, 움직이다

permanent 영구적인, 영속하는

attach 붙이다, 첨부하다, 소속하다

detach 떼어내다

apply 적용하다, 적용되다, 지원하다

sneer 비웃다, 냉소하다

leather 가죽

brief 간결한, 잠시의

resolute 굳게 결심한, 단호한

refuse 거절하다, 거부하다

loan 대부, 대부금

embark 착수하다, 승선시키다.

punctual 시간을 엄수하는

repute 평판, ~이라고 평하다

quality 질, 소질, 품질

possess 소유하다

disposal 처분, 처리, 배치

partial 부분적인, 편파적인

consume 소비하다, 다 써버리다

vast 엄청난, 막대한, 거대한

audience 청중

auditorium 강당, 방청석

audible 들을 수 있는, 들리는

inaudible 들을 수 없는

whisper 속삭이다, 속삭임

watchful 주의 깊은

tender 부드러운, 연한, 다정다감한

cradle 요람, 발상지

treasure 보물, 보배

solitude 고독

guard 지키다, 보호하다

thieve 훔치다

raid 습격, 공습, 침입, 기습

worth ~의 가치가 있는

estimation 평가, 판단

fare 운임, 요금

enormous 엄청난, 거대한

curious 호기심이 강한,

plague 역병, 전염병

perish 죽다, 사멸하다, 멸망하다

starvation 아사, 기아, 궁핍

poverty 가난, 빈곤

condemn 비난하다

invade 침략하다, 침입하다

concentration 집중, 집결

centralize 집중시키다

centrifugal 원심력의

eccentric 이상한, 낯선,

stride 활보, 성큼성큼 걷다

slight 근소한, 약간의, 경미한

principle 원리, 원칙, 주의

principal 주요한, 제일의, 교장

primitive 원시의, 초기의, 태고의

race 인종, 민족, 경주

discriminate 식별하다, 차별하다

prohibit 금지하다, 방해하다

impose 부과하다, 강요하다

protest 항의하다, 주장하다, 항의

malice   악의, 원한
accompany   동반하다, 동행하다
courteous   공손한, 예의바른
capricious   변덕스러운, 변화무쌍한
physician   내과 의사, 의사
cure   고치다, 치료하다
oath   맹세, 서약
competition   경쟁, 경기, 경쟁자
athlete   운동선수
deliberate   신중한
severe   엄격한, 심한
harsh   거친, 가혹한, 엄한
discipline   규율, 훈련
atmosphere   환경, 분위기
tension   긴장, 긴박
conduct   행동하다, 지도하다
region   지역, 지방
survey   조사하다, 둘러 보다
broadcast   방송하다, 방영하다
satisfy   만족시키다
embrace   포옹하다, 껴안다
scheme   계획, 사업 계획, 음모
devise   고안하다
visible   눈에 보이는, 명백한
vision   시력, 통찰력, 환상
visual   시각의, 눈에 보이는
advise   충고하다
evidence   증거, 증인
provide   준비하다, 대비하다
supervise   감독하다, 지휘하다
revise   개정하다, 변경하다

paralyze   마비시키다
tragic   비극적인, 비참한
abrupt   갑작스러운
embarrass   당황하게 하다
dreadful   무서운, 두려운
frustrate   좌절시키다
facility   쉬움, 설비, 편의 시설
huge   거대한
bright   빛나는, 밝은, 영리한
aspire   열망하다, 갈망하다
aware   ~을 알고 있는
irritable   화를 잘 내는, 민감한
intensive   강한, 강인한, 철저한
precede   앞장서다, 앞서다, 우선하다
incessant   끊임없는, 부단한
exceed   초과하다, (한도를) 넘다
succeed   성공하다, 계승하다,
concede   양보하다, 승인하다
treason   반역, 반역죄
treacherous   배반하는, 반역하는
entreat   간청하다, 탄원하다
traitor   반역자, 배신자
plot   음모, 책략
sacrifice   희생(물), 희생시키다
compulsory   강제적인, 의무적인
dilemma   진퇴양난, 딜레마, 궁지
moral   도덕적인, 윤리의
witness   목격하다, 목격자, 증언
trial   시도, 시련, 재판
testify   증언하다, 증명하다
miracle   기적

steep 가파른, 경사가 급한
castle 성, 성곽
luxury 사치, 사치품
discreet 분별력 있는, 신중한
tremendous 무서운, 무시무시한
engage 약속하다, 약혼하다
minister 장관, 성직자
commercial 상업상의, 통상의
appropriate 적당한, 적절한
comment 논평, 비평하다, 논평하다
secretary 비서
arrange 가지런히 하다, 배열하다
belonging 소지품, 소유물
value 가치, 값어치, 진가
publish 발표하다, 출판하다
tax 세금, 부담을 지우다
article 기사, (법령 등의) 조항
approximate 대략의, 근사한, 거의
replace ~에 대신하다, 대체하다
accomplish 이루다, 성취하다
numerous 다수의, 무수히 많은
rare 진귀한, 드문
gloomy 우울한, 음울한
countenance 표정, 안색
leap 껑충 뛰다, 도약하다
moderately 알맞게, 적당히
clumsy 볼품없는, 어색한, 서투른
mobile 이동할 수 있는
slender 호리호리한, 날씬한
intimate 친밀한, 친숙한
sanitary 위생적인, 위생의

chief 우두머리, 지배자, 장관
panic 공포, (경제) 공황
avenge 보복하다, 복수하다
seizure 붙잡음, 체포, 압류, 몰수
investigate 조사하다, 연구하다
liberal 자유로운, 자유주의의
venerate 존경하다, 숭배하다
sage 현인, 성인, 슬기로운, 현명한
nod (머리를) 끄덕이다
homage 경의, 존경
gather 모으다, 모이다
loyal 충성스러운, 성실한
royalty 왕위, 왕권, 특허권 사용료
splendid 훌륭한, 화려한
include 포함하다, 함유하다
collect 모으다, 수집하다
recollect 회상하다
elect 선출하다, 선택하다
select 선택하다, 선발하다
candidate 후보자, 지원자
swear 맹세하다, 선서하다
barren 불모의, 불임의
shabby 초라한, 낡아빠진, 지저분한
forbear 참다, 견디다
insult 모욕하다, 모욕
insolent 건방진, 오만한
subject 백성, 부하, 주제
flood 홍수, 범람, 범람시키다
subside 가라앉다, 침전하다
painful 아픈, 고통을 주는, 괴로운
descend 내려가다, 감소하다
ascend 오르다, 상승하다

landscape 풍경, 경치
renowned 유명한
outstanding 눈에 띄는, 현저한,
award (상을) 수여하다, 시상
compensation 배상, 보상, 갚음
fault 결점, 과실, 잘못, 실수
entire 완전한, 전체의
admit 인정하다, 허가하다
abandon 포기하다, 그만두다
fatal 숙명적인, 치명적인
refer 언급하다
contemptuous 경멸적인
obvious 명백한, 분명한, 두드러진
resent 분개하다
sensible 분별 있는, 느낄 수 있는
sensitive 느끼기 쉬운, 민감한
sentiment 감정, 정서, 감상
consent 동의하다
assent 동의하다, 동의, 찬성
still 조용한, 정지한, 아직, 여전히
beast 짐승
plead 탄원하다, 변호하다
mercy 자비, 인정, 용서
appeal 호소하다, 간청하다
fund 자금, 기금
scarce 부족한, 적은, 모자라는, 드문
alter 바꾸다, 수정하다
abnormal 비정상의, 이상한, 변칙의
normal 정상의, 보통의
cultivate 경작하다, 기르다
irrigate 관개하다, 물을 끌어 대다
administer 경영하다, 관리하다

passive 수동적인, 소극적인
naughty 장난꾸러기의, 행실이 못된
deprive 빼앗다, 박탈하다
miser 구두쇠, 수전노
fortune 재산, 운, 행운
punish 처벌하다, 벌하다
inevitable 피할 수 없는
indignant 분개한, 성난
vulgar 저속한, 통속적인
apologize 사과하다, 변명하다
awful 무서운, 끔직한
dismal 음침한, 음울한
twilight 환혼, 어스름, 여명, 쇠퇴기
peer 응시하다, 동료, 귀족
pensive 생각에 잠긴, 슬픈
gaze 응시하다, 뚫어지게 보다
architecture 건축술, 건축학
apprehend 이해하다
tribe 종족, 부족
savage 야만적인, 미개한, 잔인한
notorious 악명 높은
politician 정치가
shrewd 약삭빠른, 영리한
deceive 속이다, 기만하다
complicate 복잡하게 하다
complex 복잡한
apparatus 기구, 기계
experiment 실험
diminish 감소하다, 줄이다
minimum 최소의
maximum 최고점, 최대의, 극대의

conceive 상상하다, 마음에 품다

hardly 거의 ~않다

disgust 혐오감, 넌더리나게 하다

grief 슬픔, 비탄

tame 길들어진, 유순한

pertinent 적절한, 적당한, 관계있는

pet 애완동물

wicked 사악한, 나쁜, 심술궂은

astonishing 놀라운, 눈부신

variety 다양성, 변화

subtle 민감한, 미묘한

approach 접근하다, 접근

vacuum 진공, 진공의

vacant 빈, 공허한

evacuate 피신시키다

fume 연기, 김, 증기, 연기가 나다

spill 엎지르다, 흘리다

chemistry 화학

miniature 소형의, 축소 모형

minute 미세한, 하찮은, 아주 작은

tiny 작은, 조그마한

scratch 긁다, 할퀴다

queer 기묘한, 괴상한

nightmare 악몽, 무서운 일

wretched 비참한, 불쌍한

trap 덫, 올가미, 함정, 덫으로 잡다, (함정이나 속임수 등에)말려들게 하다

timid 겁 많은, 소심한

firm 굳은, 단단한, 회사

confirm 확실하게 하다, 확인하다

chemical 화학의, 화학적인

drift 표류하다, 떠내려가다

toxic 유독한, 중독성의

intoxicate 취하게 하다, 흥분시키다

triumph 승리, 정복, 대성공

adversity 역경, 불운

cancel 취소하다, 중지하다

gorgeous 화려한, 호화스러운

bride 신부

dumb 벙어리의, 우둔한

sullen 부루퉁한, 음울한, 시무룩한

reluctant 싫어하는

tranquil 조용한, 고요한

dreary 음침한, 음울한, 적막한

fruitless 결실 없는

exertion 노력

deplore 비탄하다, 개탄하다

trait 특성, 특질

personality 개성, 성격

qualify 자격을 주다, 권한을 주다

dialect 방언, 사투리

genuine 순종의, 진짜의

scrutinize 면밀히 조사하다

traffic 교통, 통행

stick 막대기, 붙이다, 찌르다

bold 대담한, 용감한, 과감한

defiance 도전, 무시, 반항

despite ~임에도 불구하고(=in spite of, notwithstanding)

slip 미끄러지다, 슬립(여자 속옷)

gradual 점진적인, 점차적인

justice 정의

justify 정당화하다

adjust 조정하다, 순응시키다, 맞추다

adjustment 조정, 순응, 적응

lofty 매우 높은, 숭고한

ignoble 비천한, 비열한, 멸시할 만한

coward 겁쟁이, 비겁한 사람, 비겁한

cowardly 비겁한 cowardice 비겁

temper 기질, 성질

peculiar 독특한, 고유의, 특별한

perceive 지각하다, 인지하다

book 예약하다, 책

favorite 마음에 드는, 매우 좋아하는, 특히 좋아하는 사람(물건)

reform 개정하다, 수정하다

radical 급진적인, 근본적인, 과격한

mission 임무, 사절단, 전도, 미션

permit 허락하다, 허가하다

omit 생략하다, ~을 빠뜨리다

submit 복종시키다, 제출하다

tremendous 무서운, 거대한, 굉장한

monster 괴물, 도깨비

trepidation 공포, 전율

view 경치, ~라고 생각하다

magnificent 웅장한, 장대한, 훌륭한

magnitude 크기, 양, 중대성

magnanimous 관대한, 도량이 큰

magnify 확대하다, 과장하다

ravage 파괴, 황폐, 파괴하다

undergo 겪다, 경험하다

frugal 부족한, 절약하는, 검소한

scant 부족한, 빈약한, 모자라는

modify 변경하다, 수정하다

formal 공식적인, 형식적인

cooperation 협력, 협동

warrant 보증, 보증하다

obstacle 방해, 장애(물)

surmount 극복하다

fortitude 굳세고 용감함, 꿋꿋함

applaud 박수갈채를 보내다

tedious 지루한, 지겨운, 진저리나는

overcome 극복하다, 이기다

vigor 활기, 원기, 정력

amuse 재미나게 하다

satellite 위성, 인공위성

miss 그리워하다, 놓치다

transmit 보내다, 전송하다

emit (빛 등을) 내다, 발산하다

emission 방사, 발산

dismiss 해고하다, 면직시키다

blame 비난, 비난하다, 책임

greed 욕심, 탐욕

colony 식민지, 거류지

disclose 드러내다, 폭로하다

desperate 절망적인, 자포자기의

siege 포위공격

violation 위반, 침해

misery 고통, 비참함, 불행

endure 견디다, 참다, 인내하다

dizzy 현기증 나는, 어지러운
repeat 되풀이하다
abuse 남용하다, 학대하다
official 공식적인, 공무적인, 공무원
nationality 국적
bid 명령하다, 말하다
robust 건장한, 튼튼한
selfish 이기적인
disregard 무시하다, 경시하다, 무시
heritage 유산, 상속 재산
inherit 물려받다, 상속하다
heir 상속인, 후계자
heredity 유전
alert 방심 않는, 경계하는, 경계
rigid 엄격한, 완고한, 단단한
soul 정신, 영혼
tumultuous 소란스러운, 동요하는
banish 추방하다, 내쫓다
disperse 흩어지게 하다, 퍼뜨리다
urban 도시의, 도시 특유의
revolt 반란, 폭동, 반란을 일으키다
reign 통치, 군림, 통치하다,
supreme 최고로, 최고의
will 의지
instruct 가르치다, 통고하다, 알리다
cordial 진심에서 우러난
sermon 설교
honesty 정직
deliver 배달하다, 넘겨주다

allure 유혹하다, 유인하다, 유혹
role 배역, 역할, 임무, 할 일
prominent 두드러진, 현저한
fraud 사기, 기만, 사기꾼
elaborate 공들인, 정교한
labor 노동, 노동하다
manual 손의, 손으로 하는, 소책자
manage 경영하다, 관리하다, 다루다
manufacture 제조, 제품, 제조 공업
emancipate (노예 등을) 해방하다
manuscript 손으로 쓴, 원고, 사본
employ 고용하다
revere 존경하다, 숭배하다
genius 천재, 귀재, 천재적 재능
evil 나쁜, 사악한, 악, 죄악
addict 중독 시키다
confront 직면하다, 맞서다
tendency 경향, 추세, 성향
vain 헛된, 허영심이 강한
exaggerate 과장하다
swift 신속한, 눈 깜짝할 사이의
reply 응답, 대답, 대답하다
trivial 시시한, 하찮은
infection 전염, 감염
heal (상처, 고장, 아픔 등을) 고치다
sorrow 슬픔, 비애, 비탄, 슬퍼하다
stumble 비틀거리며 걷다
stout 뚱뚱한, 튼튼한
languid 나른한, 활기가 없는

figure 숫자, 인물, 그림, 계산하다
quote 인용하다
pious 경건한, 신앙심이 깊은, 독실한
indifferent 무관심한, 중요치 않은
curse 저주하다
humble 겸손한, 비천한
potent 강력한, 세력 있는, 유력한
kindle 불붙이다, 태우다, 자극하다
utter 발언하다, 전적인, 완전한
utterly 완전히, 순전히, 아주
mechanical 기계의, 기계적인
crash 충돌하다
simultaneous 동시에 일어나는
simulate 가장하다, ~인 체 하다
assimilate 동화하다
similar 같은, 유사한
decent 고상한, 꽤 좋은, 점잖은
narrate 설명하다, 이야기하다
declare 선언하다, 공표하다,
intentional 고의의, 계획된
menace 협박하다, 협박, 위협
prudent 신중한, 분별 있는
withdraw 철수시키다, 인출하다
grin 이를 드러내고 히죽 웃다
mourn 슬퍼하다, 한탄하다,
transient 덧없는, 일시적인
casual 우연의, 무심결의, 평상복의
casualty 사상자, 부상자, 불상사
ceremony 의식, 식, 의례, 형식
harm 해, 손해, 손상
actually 실제로, 사실은, 참으로

feminine 여자의, 여성의
welfare 복지, 번영, 행복, 건강함
concerned 걱정스러운, 염려하는
wage 임금, 품삯
annual 1년의, 해마다의
survive 살아남다
drain 배수(방수)하다, (힘, 재물 등을) 차츰 소모시키다, 고갈시키다
struggle 분투하다, 싸우다
alliance 동맹, 연맹
inhibit 억제하다, 금지하다
factor 요소, 요인, 인자
crucial 결정적인, 중대한
attorney 변호사, 대리인
betray 누설하다, 배반하다
reveal 폭로하다, 누설하다
resolute 굳게 결심한, 단호한
admire 숭배하다, 칭찬하다
optimist 낙천주의자
pessimist 염세주의자, 비관론자
discern 식별하다, 분간하다,
astounding 몹시 놀라게 하는
widow 미망인, 과부
pale 창백한, 핏기 없는, 희미한
cease 그만두다, 중지하다, 멈추다
hostile 적의 있는, 적대하는
puzzle 수수께끼, 당황하게 하다
preach 설교하다, 전도하다
timber 재목, 목재
conspire 공모하다, 음모를 꾸미다
eliminate 제거하다, 삭제하다

stain 얼룩, 때, 더럽히다
dawn 새벽, 여명, 날이 새다
haughty 오만한, 거만한
pierce 꿰뚫다, 관통하다, 찌르다
gain 얻다, 획득하다, 이익, 증진
germ 세균, 병원균
multiply 증가시키다, 늘다, 곱하다
multitude 다수, 군중
multiplicity 다수, 다양성
multiple 다수의, 복식의, 복합적인
analyze 분석하다, 분해하다
copper 구리, 동전
content 내용물, 차례, 목록, 만족한
fine 벌금, 과태료, 벌금을 과하다
verse 운문, 시, 시구
prose 산문, 산문체
poet 시인
mutual 서로의, 공동의
background 배경, 바탕
outlook 조망, 경치, 견해, 전망, 전도
riddle 수수께끼, 난문
foster 기르다, 조장하다, 양육하다
throb (심장이) 뛰다, 고동치다
shake 흔들다, 잡아 흔들다
futile 효과 없는, 쓸데없는
recommend 추천하다, 천거하다
reasonable 합리적인, 사리를 아는
alternative 양자택일, 대안, 대안의
implore 탄원하다, 간청하다
forgive 용서하다, 눈감아주다
republic 공화국, 공화 정체

crude 천연 그대로의, 조잡한
vertical 수직의, 정점의, 세로의
horizon 지평선, 수평선
vehicle 운송 수단, 탈 것, 차량
sterile 불모의, 불임의, 생산 못하는
rely 의지하다, 신뢰하다, 믿다
prosper 번영하다, 번창하다
divide 나누다, 쪼개다, 분할하다
reap 수확하다
ridiculous 웃기는, 우스꽝스러운
rear 뒤, 후미, 후방의, 기르다
pasture 목장, 목초지
carve 새기다, 베다, 조각하다
mature 성숙한, 원숙한, 익은
inhabit ~에 살다, 거주하다
decade 10년, 10개가 한 벌이 된 것
assign 할당하다, 배당하다
worship 숭배, 예배, 참배, 존경
absurd 어리석은, 불합리한
frame 벼대, 구조, 틀, 테두리
account 계산, 계산서, (예금) 계좌
torture 고문, 심한 고통, 고뇌
torment 고통, 고뇌, 고문
reject 거절하다
realm 왕국, 범위, 영역
debate 논쟁하다, 토론하다
dispute 논쟁하다, 토의하다
vex 괴롭히다, 성가시게 굴다
remove 옮기다, 이전하다, 제거하다
mix 혼합하다, 섞다
reprove 꾸짖다, 책망하다, 비난하다

scorn 경멸, 조소하다

debt 빚, 채무

immense 거대한, 막대한,

pregnancy 임신

specimen **표본**

occasional 이따끔의

gigantic 거인 같은,

stem 줄기, 유래하다

singular 특이한, 유일한

convince 확신시키다

jury 배심원

shortage 부족, 결핍,

animate ~에 생기 있게 하다

accustom 익히다

destination 목적지, 목적

destiny 운명

trifle 하찮은 것, 사소한

anticipate 예상하다

extremity 맨 끝, 극도

dwell 살다, 거주하다

remote 먼, 멀리 떨어진

courageous 용기 있는,

awkward 어색한, 서투른

yield 생산하다, 보하다

withhold 보류하다, 억제하다

vote 투표하다, 투표, 투표권

quit 그만두다, 중지하다, 끊다

pursuit 추구, 추적

ruthless 무자비한, 냉정한

enable ~할 수 있게 하다

raw 날것의, 가공치 않은

thrive 영하다, 무성해

abolish 폐지하다

penalty 형벌, 벌금

promotion 진급, 승진

demotion 강등, 좌천, fulfil (약속
등)이행하다

duty 의무, 임무

oblige 어쩔 수 없이 ~하게 하다,
억지로 시키다

polite 공손한, 예의 바른

ordeal 시련, 괴로운 체험

soar 높이 치솟다

remedy 치료, 요법

yearn 그리워하다

empire 제국, 왕국

withstand 견디어내다

vow 맹세, 맹세하다

utmost 최대의, 최고의,

utility 유용, 유익,

prior 보다 중요한

trustworthy **믿을 수 있는**

sword 검, 칼, 무력

rural 시골의, 전원의

quaint 기이한, 기묘한, 진기한

purpose 목적, 취지, 의도

overtake 따라잡다, 앞지르다

symmetry (좌우의) 대칭, 균형

striking 현저한, 두드러진

ruthless 무자비한, 냉정한

rascal   악한, 불량배

myriad   일만의, 무수한

livelihood   살림, 생계

invert   거꾸로 하다, 전도시키다

convert   변하게 하다, 전환하다

formula   판에 박은 말, 형식, 방식, 공식

hygiene   위생, 위생학

grumble   투덜거리다, 불평하다

fuel   연료, 에너지, 연료를 공급하다

extravagant   도가 지나친, 낭비하는

durable   영속성 있는, 오래 견디는

interfere   방해하다, 훼방하다, 간섭하다

craft   기능, 교활, 비행기, 우주선

burden   무거운 짐, 부담, 의무, 책임

staff   직원, 참모, 간부

initial   처음의, 낱말 첫머리에 있는

aviation   비행, 항공, 비행기

pioneer   개척자, 선구자, 개척하다

wither   시들다, 말라죽게 하다

volume   책, 권, 부피, 음량(볼륨)

shelf   선반

usher   (극장, 교회 등의) 안내인

wealth   부, 재산.

nourish   영양분을 주다, 기르다

nutrition   영양물, 영양물 섭취

essence   본질, 정수, 진수

recover   되찾다, 회복하다

myth   신화, 전설

lurk   숨다, 잠적하다, 잠복하다

juvenile   소년의, 젊은, 소년, 소녀

drudgery   고된 일, 하기 싫은 일

counsel   상담하다, 조언하다, 상담, 의논

brisk   활발한, 상쾌한, 기분 좋은

average   평균, 표준

wistful   탐내는, 바라는, 그리워하는

trim   (머리, 잔디 등을 깎아) 다듬다, 정돈하다, 손질하다

hedge   산울타리, 울타리, 장벽

swell   부풀다, 팽창하다

rumor   소문, 유언비어

purchase   사다, 구매, 구입

overlook   내려다 보다, 못 보고 지나치다, 대충 보다

notion   관념, 개념, 생각, 의향

vague   막연한, 모호한, 애매한

propose   제안하다, 제의하다

muscle   근육

lift   들어 올리다, 올리다

limit   한계, 한정하다, 제한하다

tolerate   참다, 견디다, 관대하게 다루다

intrude   침입하다, 강요하다, 참견하다

realize   깨닫다, 실감하다, 이해하다

humiliate   굴욕감을 느끼게 하다

furnish   공급하다, 가구를 설비하다

issue   문제, 논점, 발행하다

hypothesis   가설, 가정

guarantee   보증, 보증하다

furniture   가구

antique   고풍의, 고대의, 고물, 골동품

antedate   앞선 날짜로 하다

anterior   선행한, 보다 이전의

extract   뽑아내다, 추출하다

attract   매혹하다, 끌어당기다

contract   계약

distract   (주의를) 딴 데로 돌리다,

abstract   추상적인, 추출하다, 뽑아내다

shelter   피난처, 은신처, 대피호

glance   흘긋 봄, 일견(—瞥)

vocation   천직, 직업

upset   뒤엎다, 당황하게 하다

trace 자취, 발자국

upright 똑바로 선, 수직의, 정직한

trespass 침입하다, 침해하다

sue 고소하다

reward 보수, 보상

surround 둘러싸다, 에워싸다, 포위하다

provoke 화나게 하다, 자극하다

adornment 꾸미기, 장식, 장식품

navy 해군

mo(u)ld 주조하다, 틀에 부어 만들다,

lessen 적어지게 하다, 줄이다

intricate 얽힌, 복잡한

interrogate 심문하다, 질문하다

hindrance 방해, 장애, 방해물

grasp 붙잡다, 파악하다, 이해하다

still 아직, 조용한, 정지한, 움직이지 않는

fundamental 기본적인, 근본적인, 필수의,

expose 드러내다, 폭로하다, 진열하다

suspend 매달다, 중지시키다

depend 의존하다, 종속되다

pendulum (시계 따위의) 추, 진자

append 첨가하다, 첨부하다

dispense 분배하다, 없이 지내다(with)

perpendicular 수직의, 직립한, 수직의

straw 짚, 밀짚, 스트로, 빨대

introduce 소개하다, 들여 도다

holy 신성한, 성스러운, 거룩한

greet 인사하다

funeral 장례의, 장례식

external 외부의, 외계의, 밖의

drastic 격렬한, 맹렬한, 철저한

correspond 일치하다, 부합하다

draft 도안, 설계도, 징병, 초안을 잡다,
 선발하다

cope 겨루다, 맞서다, 대처하다

bond 속박, 묶는 것, 채권, 본드

ideal 이상, 숭고한 목표(원리), 공상, 이
 상의, 이상적인

astronaut 우주 비행사

astronomy 천문학

astrology 점성술

astroid 불가사리, 소행성

disaster 재앙, 불행, 재난

wellbeing 행복, 안녕, 복지

benefit 이익, 이롭다, 이익을 얻다(from)

beneficial 유익한, 이로운

benefactor 은혜를 베푸는 사람, 은인

benediction 축복, 은총

benign 친절한, 온화한

uphold 받치다, 지탱하다, 지지하다,

tremble 떨다, 떨리다, 진동하다

surrender 항복하다

option 선택권, 취사 택

proportion 비율, 비, 비례, 균형, 몫

origin 기원, 태생

orientation 방침, 적응, 적응 지도

expense 소비, 지출, 경비

right 권리, 옳은, 바른, 오른쪽의

pulse 맥박, 파동, 진동

output 생산, 생산고, 출력

notable 주목할 만한, 두드러진, 유명한

trend 경향, 방향, 유행, 추세

monument 기념비, 기념물, 유물

liable ~하기 쉬운

navigation 항해, 항공
equipment 장비, 비품, 설비, 준비
instrument 기계, 기구, 도구, 악기
moisture 습기, 수증기, 수분
legitimate 합법적인, 정당한
legislate 법률을 제정하다
legal 합법적인, 법률의
legislature 입법부
interpret 해석하다, 설명하다
defense 방어, 수비
heretic 이교도, 이단자
advocate 옹호하다, 변호하다
vocal 소리의, 구두의
evoke 일깨우다, 불러일으키다
revoke 취소하다, 폐지하다
voice 목소리
vocabulary 어휘, 단어집
grant 승인하다, 허가하다, 허가,
frivolous 경박한, 천박한, 하찮은
incline (마음이) 내키게 하다
exploit 개발하다, 착취하다, 공적,
species (분류상의) 종, 종류, 형식
mode 방법, 양식, 유행
department 부서, 매장, 학부, 과
legend 전설, 위인전
interest 이익, 이자, 흥미, 관심
bloom 꽃, 꽃이 피다, 번영하다
devil 악마, 마귀
thoroughly 완전히, 철저하게
subjective 주관적인, 주격(S)
criterion (판단, 비판의) 표준, 기준

doom 운명, 파멸, 운명 짓다
convey (물건, 승객 등을) 나르다
breakdown 고장, 파손, 붕괴, 몰락
boast 자랑하다, 자랑하며 말하다
astray 길을 잃어, 못된 길에 빠져
weary 피곤한, 싫증이 난
undertake 떠맡다, 착수하다
transparent 투명한, (직물 등이) 비
치어 보이는, 명백한
transition 변천, 변화, 과도기
allot 할당하다, 배분하다, 분배하다
surplus 나머지, 잔여, 과잉
wheat 밀, 소맥
surpass ～보다 낫다, 능가하다
dignity 존엄, 위엄, 근엄
reverse 역, 반대의, 거꾸로 하다
prophecy 예언
organ 기관, 장기, (정부 등의) 기관
native 출생지의
bone 뼈
plow (밭을) 갈다, 경작하다
avail 유용하다, 도움이 되다
wholesome 건강에 좋은, 건전한
vanish 사라지다, 없어지다
graduation 졸업식, 졸업, 학위 획득
free 면제된, 무료의, 자유의
explanation 설명, 해석
donation 기부, 기증
convention 집회, 모임, 관습, 전통
subdue 정복하다, 진압하다
delight 기쁨, 매우 기쁘게 하다

genial 온화한, 따뜻한

alien 외국의, 외래의, 외계인

foundation 기초

expedition 탐험, 탐험대

arctic 북극의, 북극

exotic 외국의, 이국적인

domain 영토, 구역

polar 극지방의, 남(북)극의

contrive 고안하다, 연구해 내다

calculate 계산하다, 추정하다

beware 경계하다, 조심하다

offer 제공하다, 제출하다, 제안하다

ashamed 부끄러워, 수줍어하는

tomb 묘지

summary 요약, 요약한

resort 놀이터, (수단에) 의존하다

demon 악마, 마귀, 귀신

prompt 신속한, 즉시의, 자극하다

omen 징조, 징후, 불길한 예감

might 힘, 강한

laboratory 연구소, 실험실

insight 통찰력

hasty 서두르는, 성급한

conclude 결정하다, 결말짓다

include 포함하다

exclude 제외시키다, 배제하다

layer 층, 쌓은 것, 놓는(쌓는) 사람

intercourse 교제, 왕래, 교통

heedless 부주의한, 조심성 없는

glacier 빙하

mass 큰 덩어리, 모임

iceberg 빙산, 빙하

seclude 격리시키다

disclose 노출시키다, 폭로하다

enclose 둘러싸다, 에워싸다

contact 접촉, 연락, 맞닿음

reaction 반작용, 반응, 반항

generous 관대한, 너그러운

forsaken 버려진, 유기된

appear 나타나다,

exhibit 전시하다, 보이다

doctrine 학설, 주의

contrast 대조하다, 대조를 이루다

contrary 반대의, 정 반대

bestow 주다, 수여하다

ascribe ~의 탓으로 돌리다

timely 때맞춘, 적절한 시간의

suburban 교외의

reserve 보존하다, 예약하다, 사양

prolong 연장하다, 연기하다

proficient 숙달된, 능숙한

offspring 자식, 자손

gene 유전자, 유전 인자

generate 발생시키다, 낳다

degenerate 퇴보하다, 변질하다

assume 추정하다, 생각하다

warfare 전쟁

transform 변형시키다

superficial 표면상의, 외면의

propagate 선전하다, 보급시키다

orbit (천체의)궤도

mock 흉내 내다, 조롱하다

petulant 성미 급한, 성 잘 내는

armament 군대, 군사력, 군비

genetics 유전학

metropolis 수도, 중심지

initial 처음의, 머리문자

inherent 고유의, 타고난

hardy 단단한, 튼튼한

generalization 일반화, 보편화

forlorn 고독한, 쓸쓸한, 버림받은

exempt 면제된, 면제하다

divine 신의, 신성한, 예언하다

dictation 구술, 받아쓰기, 명령

dictator 독재자, 받아쓰게 하는 사람

benedict 축복하다

dictionary 사전

dedicate 헌납하다, (생애를) 바치다

contradict 반박하다, 모순되다

indicate 지시하다, 지적하다

predict 예언하다, 예보하다

bend 구부리다, (노력을) 기울이다

ascertain ~을 확인하다

float (물 위에) 띄우다

frank 솔직한, 명백한

dominant 지배적인, 통치력 있는

controversy 논쟁, 논의

bless 축복하다

mine 광산, 채굴하다

last 계속하다, 마지막의

haunt 자주가다, 출몰하다다

leper 나병환자, 문둥이

contend 다투다, 싸우다, 주장하다

biology 생물학

biography 전기, 일대기

sound 건전한, 소리, 처럼 들리다

tide 조수, 조류, 흥망성쇠

thrift 검소, 절약

suffrage 투표, 선거권

sublime 장엄한, 숭고한, 탁월한

resemblance 유사, 닮음

profess 공언하다, 고백하다

oral 구두의, 구술의, 입의

consult 상담하다

merchandise 상품, 제품, 매매하다

merchant 상인

afflict 괴롭히다, (고통을) 가하다

inflict (구타 등을) 가하다, 괴롭히다

superior 뛰어난, ~보다 나은

hardship 고난, 곤란

game 사냥감, 놀이, 게임

forbid 금하다, 금지하다

folly 어리석은 행동, 어리석음

excel 능가하다, ~보다 낫다

assertion 주장, 단언

tool 연장, 공구, 수단

fix 고정시키다, 수리하다

summit 정상, 꼭대기, 정상급

resume 다시 시작하다

exactly 정확하게, 조금도 틀림없이

ethics 윤리학

divide 나누다, 쪼개다, 분할하다

diverse 다양한, 여러 가지의의

continent 대륙, 육지

autobiography 자서전

arrogant 거만한, 오만한

stern 엄격한, 단호한

structure 건물, 구조, 구성

repent 후회하다, 뉘우치다

sin 죄, 죄악, 잘못

regret 후회하다, 후회, 유감

accommodate 숙박시키다

presume 추정하다, 가정하다,

preface 머리말, 서문

accord 일치, 조화, 조화하다

melancholy 우울, 우울한

meditate 숙고하다, 명상하다

incurable 불치의, 고칠 수 없는

accumulate 축적하다, 쌓다, 모으다

geometry 기하학

barometer 기압계

speedometer 속도계

symmetry 좌우 대칭, 균형

thermometer 온도계

accuracy 정확, 정확도

theory 이론, 학설

stroll 한가로이 거닐다, 방랑하다

strict 엄한, 엄밀한

strife 투쟁, 싸움, 경쟁

reproach 꾸짖다, 책망하다, 비난

prodigal 낭비하는, 방탕한

prey 먹이, 희생, 밥

hawk 매

strip (껍질, 겉옷 등을) 벗기다

digest 소화하다, 간추리다

abide by 고수하다, 지키다

renounce 포기하다, 단념하다

bait 미끼, 유혹하다

precise 정확한, 정밀한

strenuous 분투적인, 열심인,

pray 빌다, 기원하다

barbaric 야만의, 미개한

strain 긴장시키다, 잡아당기다, 긴
장, 팽팽함, 큰 부담

rejoice 기뻐하다, 기쁘게 하다

praise 칭찬, 칭찬하다

means 수단, 방법, 재산, 부

store 저장, 저장하다, 가게

barrier 장벽, 장애물

meager 빈약한, 메마른, 야윈

clue 실마리, 단서

sting 찌르다, 자극, 침

basis 기초, 기본

theme 주제, 제목, 테마

stifle ~의 숨을 막다, 질식시키다,
억누르다, 억제하다

beckon (손짓 따위로) 부르다, 신호
하다

occur 머리에 떠오르다, 생각이 나
다, 발생하다

mention 언급하다, 말하다

indulge 빠지다, 탐닉하다,

induce 권유하다, 야기하다

indolent 게으른, 나태한

halt 멈추다, 멈추게 하다, 정지

folk 사람들, 가족, 친척

focus   초점, 초점을 맞추다

eternal   영원한, 끝없는

flourish 번창하다, 번영하다,

calling   직업, 천직

steer   ~의 키를 잡다, 조종하다

cancer   암

propel   추진하다, 나아가게 하다

expel   내쫓다, 쫓아버리다, 추방하다

dispel   쫓아버리다, 없애다

repel   쫓아버리다, 격퇴하다

impel   억지로 ~시키다, 추진하다

compel   억지로 ~시키다, 강요하다

capable   ~할 수 있는, 유능한

stately   위엄 있는, 장엄한

register   등록하다, 기재하다

potential   잠재하는, 잠재력이 있는

career   경력, 생애

maxim   격언, 금언

inborn   타고난, 선천적인

talent   재능

staple   주요한, 중요한, 주요 산물

standpoint   견지, 관점, 견해

catastrophe   재난, 재앙, 대단원

taint   더럽히다, 오염시키다, 감염

detest   혐오하다, 매우 싫어하다

abundant   풍부한, 부유한

prevail   이기다, 우세하다, 보급되다

observe   관찰하다, 준수하다

absorb   열중시키다, 흡수하다

accelerate   가속하다, 촉진하다

stubborn   완고한, 고집 센

esteem   존경하다, 존중하다

flexible   구부리기 쉬운, 융통성 있는

rubber   고무

caution   조심, 경계

spur   박차, 박차를 가하다, 자극하다

epoch   신기원, 신시대, 중요한 사건

flesh   살, 육체, 살점

cave   동굴

ancient   고대의, 구식의

ancestor   선조, 조상

advance   전진하다, 증진시키다

enhance   높이다, 강화하다

refresh   상쾌하게 하다, 새롭게 하다

postpone   연기하다, 뒤로 미루다

posterity   자손, 후세

spot   장소, 지점, 얼룩, 더럽히다

flaw   흠, (갈라진) 금, 결점

cell   세포, 작은 방

refrain   그만두다, 삼가다, 자제하다

portray   (인물, 풍경을) 그리다

entitle   권리(자격)를 주다

censure   비난, 비난하다

flattery   아첨

enterprise   기업, 모험적인 사업

taste   미각, 맛, 맛보다, 취향

spontaneous   자발적인, 무의식적인

beforehand   미리, 벌써

reconcile   화해시키다, 조정하다

ponder   숙고하다, 곰곰이 생각하다

inability   무능력, 무력함

spirit   정신, 마음

sober 술 취하지 않은, 제정신의
decree 명령, 법령, 명령하다
snare 덫, 올가미, 함정, 유혹하다
contemporary 동시대의, 현대의
display 전시하다, 나타내다
temporary 일시적인, 임시의
slumber 잠자다, 잠
phase 국면, 양상, 현상, 상태
impudent 뻔뻔스러운, 건방진
fever 열, 열병, 흥분(상태)
district 구역, 지역, 지방
acquaint 알리다, 기별하다
coarse 조잡한, 거친, 상스러운
defect 결점, 결함, 단점
encounter (우연히) 만나다, 마주치다
feudal 봉건적인, 봉건 제도의
imprison 감옥에 넣다, 수감하다
pompous 화려한, 점잔 빼는
masterpiece 걸작, 명작, 대표작
chaos 혼돈, 무질서
sphere 구, 구형, 천체, 지구의
specialize 특수화하다, 전문화하다
sovereign 군주, 주권자, 최상의
reckless 무모한
poisonous 유독한, 독이 있는
cherish 소중히 하다, 마음에 품다
soothe 달래다, 위로하다
recall 상기하다, 생각나게 하다
plausible 그럴 듯한, 정말 같은
plain 평범한, 쉬운, 명백한, 검소한
cling 달라붙다, 매달리다, 고수하다

skill 솜씨, 숙련, 기능
sinister 불길한, 재수 없는
sincere 성실한, 진심의
petty 사소한, 보잘것없는, 작은
mankind 인류, 인간, 남성
imply 암시하다, 포함하다, 내포하다
feature 용모, 모양, 특색
disorder 무질서, 혼란
commence 개시하다, 시작하다
commodity 상품, 일용품
acute 날카로운, 뾰족한, 신랄한
persevere 인내하다, 견디어내다
adapt 적응시키다, 순응시키다,
befall (좋지 않은 일이) ~에게 일어
　　　　나다, 생기다, 들이닥치다
commonplace 평범한, 진부한, 흔해
　　　　빠진 일(이야기)
disinterested 사심 없는, 공평한
enchant 매혹하다, 요술을 걸다
shepherd 양치기, (양을) 치다
implement 도구, 이행하다
classify 분류하다, 등급으로 나누다
dare 감히 ~하다
solid 고체의, 단단한, 견고한, 고체
dense 밀집한, 빽빽한,
deal 다루다, 거래하다, 거래
sole 유일한
comfort 위안, 안락, 위로하다
meal 식사, 한 끼니(분)
scream 소리치다, 비명을 지르다
decay 부식하다, 부패하다, 타락하다

male   남자, 수컷, 남자의, 수컷의

female   여성, 암컷, 여성의, 암컷의

perplex   당황케 하다

rational   합리적인, 이성적인

rapture   황홀, 환희, 광희

shy   수줍어하는, 수줍은

aristocrat   귀족

behalf   이익, ~을 위함

contemplate   심사숙고하다

disdain   경멸하다, 멸시하다

eminent   저명한, 뛰어난, 훌륭한

feat   공적, 위업, 묘기

imperial   제국의, 황제의

majesty   위엄, 장엄, 폐하

perpetual   영구적인, 끊임없는

periodical   정기적인, 정기 간행의

peril   위험, 위태

range   범위, 구역, 열, 산맥

frequent   자주 일어나는, 빈번한

shrink   오그라들다, 움츠러지다

ardent   열렬한, 열심인, 불타는

contagion   전염, 감염, 전염병

discourse   강연, 논설, 강연하다

degrade   타락하다, (가치 등이) 떨어
지다

fame   명성

imagine   상상하다

pastime   오락, 기분전환

seek   찾다, 구하다

conceited   자부심이 강한, 자만하는

degree   정도, 학위, 등급

elastic   탄력 있는, 신축성 있는

emerge   나오다, 나타나다

bush   관목, 수풀, 덤불

fascinate   매혹하다, 넋을 빼앗다

imperative   긴급한, 필수적인

hostage   인질

release   풀어놓다, 석방하다

penetration   관통, 침투, 통과

shortcoming   결점, 단점, 부족

sacred   신성한, (신에게) 바친

appreciate   감사하다, 감상하다

embody   구체화하다, 표현하다

fantasy   공상, 환상

flash   번쩍임, 섬광

immemorial   먼 옛날의

pause   멈춤, 중지, 잠시 멈추다

separate   분리하다, 가르다

appetite   식욕, 욕망

console   위로하다, 위문하다

adequate   적당한, 충분한

complacent   자기만족의, 상냥한

defiance   도전, 반항, 무시

element   구성, 요소

fancy   공상, 좋아함

illustrate   설명하다, 예증하다

comet   혜성

trail   지나간 자국, 흔적

patent   전매특허

sentence   문장, 판결하다, 판결

adhere   들러붙다, 고수하다

comprehend   이해하다, 포함하다

conceal   숨기다, 감추다

fallacy   오류, 잘못

salute 인사하다, 경례하다

annihilate 전멸시키다, 무효로 하다

concrete 구체적인, 굳어진, 확실한

deposit 맡기다, 공탁하다, 두다

fade (빛깔이) 바래다, 사라지다

scent 향기, 냄새

adventure 모험, 모험심

advantage 유리, 이점

conservative 보수적인, 전통적인

deserve ~할 가치가 있다

faculty 능력, 재능, 전교직원

fable 우화, 전설, 지어낸 이야기

affection 사랑, 애정

negative 부정적인, 부정의하는

affirmative 긍정적인, 확언적인

consequence 결과, 중요성

detect 발견하다, 간파하다, 탐지하다

lead 납

agony 심한 고통, 번뇌, 고민

anguish 심한 고통, 번뇌, 고민

outcome 결과, 성과

anarchist 무정부주의자

congress 국회, 대의원회

determine 결심하다

imitate 모방하다

inspiration 영감

derive ~를 끌어내다, 유추하다,

perspiration 땀

wipe 닦다, 닦아 내다, 씻다

party 당파, 일행, 파티, 모임

coal 석탄

eloquent 웅변의, 능변인, 달변인

diffuse 발산하다, 퍼뜨리다

even 공평한, 짝수의, 평탄한

dye 염료, 물감, 색조, 염색하다

agriculture 농업, 농예

inalienable 양도할 수 없는

conscious 의식이 있는,

devote 헌신하다

analogous 유사한, 비슷한

ambiguous 모호한, 분명하지 않은

diameter 지름, 직경

allude 암시하다, 넌지시 말하다

algebra 대수학

confidence 신임, 신뢰, 자신, 확신

differ 다르다

discard 버리다, 해고하다

desire 바라다, 열망하다

participate (모임 등에) 참여하다

sculpture 조각

score 20, 스코어, 점수, 다수(pl.)

adolescence 청년기, 사춘기

concise 간결한, 명료한

delicious 맛있는

ecstasy 황홀, 무아지경

faith 신념, 믿음, 신앙, 성실

absolute 절대적인, 순전한

parallel 평행의, 유사한

pang 심한 고통, 양심의 가책

skeptical 회의적인, 의심 많은

admiral 해군대장, 제독

adore 숭배하다, 흠모하다, 숭앙하다

ritual 의식의, 종교적인 의식

faint 희미한, 어렴풋한, 기절한

어휘 예상 문제 (1~10회)

1. 어휘 예상 문제 (1회)

※ 다음 밑줄 친 부분에 들어갈 가장 알맞은 것을 고르시오 (1-20)

01 They decided to look for an alternative when the market was on the _____?

① wane   ② approval

③ selection   ④ assembly

02 _____ changes in the manufacturing process can lead to an increase in revenues.

① Inspective   ② Protective

③ Provisional   ④ Revolutionary

03 Regular full-time staff members accrue sick time at the rate of one paid sick day for each month worked _____ of length of service.

① alternative   ② determined

③ irrespective   ④ dependable

04 The accomplishments associated with a career in chemicals _____ the demands of the duties involved.

① create   ② find

③ outweigh   ④ process

05 If you want to _____ on a long and profitable relationship, we will supply you with various accessories and services.

① influence   ② embark

③ vary   ④ accept

06 Our Marketing Department has saved money by _____ its paper consumption.

① diminishing   ② addressing
③ increasing   ④ supporting

07 The _____ located convention centers make it easy for business travelers to attend business travelers to attend business functions in this city.

① willingly   ② absolutely
③ certainly   ④ agreeably

08 There has been _____ pressure for the chairman of the board to step down when his term ends in April.

① challenging   ② mounting
③ discharging   ④ occurring

09 The _____ documents had to be filled out again, causing a delay in the product being sent out.

① illegible   ② intentional
③ unlimited   ④ concerned

10 Matt's _____ on his work led not only to a raise, but also to a promotion within the department.

① consolidation   ② attention
③ identification   ④ concentration

11 We _____ by our all promises with a two-year warranty and a 30-day money-back guarantee.

① abide   ② follow
③ conform   ④ comply

12 The _____ employee left the office at 4 P.M. even though he still had a lot of work to do.

① completed   ② conclusive
③ absolute   ④ exhausted

13 The 2012 Improv model won wide _____ from critics at the most recent automobile show in Detroit.

① array   ② agreement
③ acclaim   ④ appeal

14 With stores across the city, Sound Wave is the _____ source for personal electronics products in Vancouver.

① selective   ② expressive
③ competitive   ④ definitive

15 T-Mobile Canada has finally decided to meet with _____ of its preposed merger with MT&T.

① opponents   ② forfeitures
③ embarkations   ④ complications

16 Janice Wolfson _____ used company funds for purposes not stipulated in the company's code of ethics.

① radically   ② necessarily
③ allegedly   ④ purposely

17 It is their _____ commitment to satisfying customers that makes BK the biggest automaker in the country.

① inconsistent   ② unwavering   ③ instant   ④ irrelevant

18 Pam and Fraser have been _____ in the kitchen staff's food supply every day recently.

① inducing   ② indulging
③ interpreting   ④ employing

19 A large _____ of the profits were reinvested into the company at the suggestion of the BOD.

① proportion   ② respondent
③ obligation   ④ statement

20 There is little doubt that government _____ in the economy is the sole way to lower unemployment.

① information   ② intervention
③ casualties   ④ supporters

[정답]

1	2	3	4	5	6	7	8	9	10
①	④	③	③	②	①	④	②	①	④
11	12	13	14	15	16	17	18	19	20
①	④	③	④	①	③	②	②	①	②

2. 어휘 예상 문제 (2회)

※ 다음 밑줄 친 부분에 들어갈 가장 알맞은 것을 고르시오. (1~20)

01 The contents of the packages are _____, so they should remain refrigerated while being shipped.

① perishable   ② affordable
③ comfortable   ④ incorrect

02 Part of the reason it has been so successful is that JD, Inc. Produces highly _____ products.

① diversified   ② authorized
③ determined   ④ decided

03 As per our new security policy, you need to _____ customers to the office when they visit.

① reform   ② demonstrate
③ reserve   ④ escort

04 Jerry is _____ having a hard time adjusting to his new position, but he will get used to it soon.

① decently   ② accurately
③ additional   ④ evidently

05 The _____ of roses greeted customers who walked into the foyer area, creating an agreeable atmosphere.

① vapor   ② odor
③ scent   ④ fume

06 Integrity is considered a very _____ quality when it comes to hiring new employees.

① desirable   ② erectable
③ seasonable   ④ permissible

07 _____ paperclips were found near Ms. Weinstein's desk earlier this afternoon.

① Complete   ② Assorted
③ Typical   ④ Inclusive

08 Laymoth Brothers has _____ the hardware store business, with more than 500 stores nationwide.

① forced   ② compelled
③ defeated   ④ dominated

09 Marcus was asked to _____ his answer into a few words and keep his comments short.

① condense   ② contract
③ commence   ④ concentrate

10 Semiconductors and microchips are more _____ to damage when exposed to high temperatures.

① unstable   ② insecure
③ delicate   ④ vulnerable

11 The development plan was _____ with fierce opposition from a few local residents.

① contended   ② confronted
③ confirmed   ④ contested

12 The advertising campaign was so successful that a majority of people say the product is now _____ recognizable.

① continuously   ② urgently
③ hastily   ④ instantly

13 The management himself welcomed the _____ guest from Germany and even hosted a lunch in their honor.

① purchased   ② sacred
③ limited   ④ distinguished

14 An _____ author sent a piece into the Times this weekend, claiming to have knowledge about an important merger.

① anonymous   ② unanimous
③ announced   ④ animated

15 The purpose of the research is to determine which metal is the most resistant to _____.

① redemption   ② corrosion
③ determination   ④ emission

16 Three board members have proved to be _____ to an agreement on the company's restructuring.

① obstacles   ② preventions
③ insinuations   ④ observances

17 According to the IT team, every way to _____ these problems involves a significant cost to the company.

① qualify   ② alter   ③ raise   ④ lessen

18 After three _____ quarters of profits, the company is once again seen as a blue-chip stock.

① successive   ② important
③ fortunate   ④ reliant

19 The interest in my savings account is not _____ at a satisfying rate.

① accounting   ② accruing
③ accosting   ④ according

20 The CEO signed an MOU on Thursday and shortly _____ held a ceremony to celebrate the event.

① later   ② soon
③ thereafter   ④ next

[정답]

1	2	3	4	5	6	7	8	9	10
①	①	④	④	③	①	②	④	①	④

11	12	13	14	15	16	17	18	19	20
②	④	④	①	②	①	④	①	②	③

3. 어휘 예상 문제 (3회)

※ 다음 밑줄 친 부분에 들어갈 가장 알맞은 것을 고르시오 (1~20)

01 My immediate boss is _____ asking me to take care of other people's day-to-day duties.

    ① painfully   ② constantly
    ③ grievously   ④ artificially

02 Rising and volatile fuel prices are _____ as a threat to the economy.

    ① perceived   ② visualized
    ③ represented   ④ deliberated

03 Unlike previous years, _____ vacation time cannot be carried over past December 31 under any circumstances.

    ① abused   ② accused
    ③ excused   ④ unused

04 The poor sales numbers are _____ of a bigger problem at Sugarloaf, Inc. than previously expected.

    ① specialized   ② indicative
    ③ reduced   ④ reserved

05 One _____ for effective executives to master is being able to delegate properly.

    ① characteristic   ② deterioration
    ③ involvement   ④ improvision

06 A _____ strike at Harty Enterprises will most likely lead to a drop in profits for the next quarter.

① observed   ② agreed
③ prolonged   ④ abused

07 The speaker was asked to _____ on his position that the economy was headed toward a recession.

① alleviate   ② elevate
③ deteriorate   ④ elaborate

08 Unfortunately, we had to _____ our agreement with Charles Hay den because of a lack of productivity.

① diagnose   ② terminate
③ inquire   ④ subcontract

09 The _____ between the rich and poor has been gradually growing in emerging economies in Asia.

① hole   ② gap
③ transit   ④ way

10 The management examined all _____ plans to increase profits.

① close   ② feasible
③ steady   ④ dependent

11 If an _____ item is offered at a lover price by a local competitor, we'll refund the difference.

① audited   ② ample
③ authorized   ④ identical

12 Employees may not park their vehicle in any area that is not specifically

_____ for parking.

① designated   ② financed
③ stationed   ④ permitted

13 The company has a zero tolerance policy for employees who _____ the rules when it comes to copyright infringement.

① grant   ② interfere
③ disconnect   ④ violate

14 There's not much hope for the pulp and paper industry in the _____ future as demand is at an all-time low.

① foreseeable   ② prevalent
③ ongoing   ④ surface

15 Janet Wiseman is _____ leaving her post because she has said she has no intention of renewing her contract.

① unbearably   ② basically
③ presumably   ④ indifferently

16 Many cutting-edge computer companies in the nation have to _____ with the possibility of breaching antitrust regulations.

① confirm   ② contact
③ contend   ④ confront

17 If you omit any of the _____ details, we will have to file the report all over again.

① decreased   ② insufficient   ③ limited   ④ incidental

18 _____ market conditions have led investors to pull their money out of stock markets in many counties.

① Unstable   ② Precious
③ Interested   ④ Lengthy

19 Experts have been trying to _____ the public's reaction to the news about Cyborg Computers' technical problems.

① generate   ② interrupt
③ gauge   ④ jeopardize

20 The board members were _____ in their decision, saying the company had to downsize at once to survive.

① unanimous   ② complete
③ utter   ④ whole

[정답]

1	2	3	4	5	6	7	8	9	10
②	①	④	②	①	③	④	②	②	②
11	12	13	14	15	16	17	18	19	20
④	①	④	①	③	③	④	①	③	①

4. 어휘 예상 문제 (4회)

※ 다음 밑줄 친 부분에 들어갈 가장 알맞은 것을 고르시오. (1~20)

01 I am planning to _____ my strategy by giving a PowerPoint presentation at the weekly sales meeting.

① illustrate ② consider
③ account ④ determine

02 When the environmental report is released later this month, it will have_____ for many companies.

① evaluations ② reservations
③ expectations ④ implications

03 Concrete is a more _____ construction material than almost anything else and is relatively inexpensive, too.

① systematic ② lateral
③ versatile ④ persistent

04 _____ use of the copy machine may result in technical difficulties, so please be careful with it.

① Extinct ② Reserved
③ Improper ④ Changeable

05 This company has more _____ resources than almost every other company in the industry.

① productive ② advantageous
③ durable ④ abundant

06 After our department's performance all last year, we suffered heavy losses during the last three months.

① extraordinary   ② vacant
③ architectural   ④ radical

07 We have relied on their keen _____ into internet marketing to develop our own Web site.

① study   ② glance
③ work   ④ insight

08 The new book on proven business models sold in excess _____ a million copies within a year of its publication.

① over   ② than
③ of   ④ to

09 Detour signs have been _____ placed on all the streets downtown that are currently undergoing construction.

① observantly   ② externally
③ importantly   ④ prominently

10 In an effort to _____ concerns about the company's ability to address shifting market demands, it hired Geoff Roberts as its CIO.

① confiscate   ② hesitate
③ function   ④ alleviate

11 Although the pool of questionnaire takers was _____ chosen, they overwhelmingly agreed on the answer to every question they were asked.

① highly   ② randomly
③ relatively   ④ cooperatively

12 Everyone agrees that we need to _____ some sophisticated marketing strategies before the end of this quarter.

① devise   ② divide
③ disrupt   ④ depart

13 The series of meetings held between the two companies resulted in the _____ of a solid business partnership.

① attempt   ② reflection
③ process   ④ cultivation

14 The board of directors was unwilling to _____ any information about its impending property acquisition decision.

① preside   ② disclose
③ arise   ④ discriminate

15 There is a lot of _____ on the part of shareholders about the company's future.

① conservation   ② automation
③ speculation   ④ integration

16 If Ms. Tompkins can sign this form, it would really help _____ the editing process.

① proceed   ② illustrate
③ describe   ④ accelerate

17 The government has started to _____ a new law regulating the import of bananas from Nicaragua.

① enforce   ② adhere   ③ associate   ④ remind

18 CDs, videos, _____, and reference materials are available for in-library use only.

① periodicals   ② review
③ check   ④ study

19 Hardwood lumber from Canada is _____ from tariffs when being exported to the United States.

① complimentary   ② privileged
③ exempt   ④ offered

20 A poll shows _____ approval of the company's new pension plan that's published on our Web site.

① widespread   ② skeptical
③ understandable   ④ uncomfortable

[정답]

1	2	3	4	5	6	7	8	9	10
①	④	③	③	④	①	④	③	④	④
11	12	13	14	15	16	17	18	19	20
②	①	④	②	③	④	①	①	③	①

5. 어휘 예상 문제 (5회)

※ 다음 밑줄 친 부분에 들어갈 가장 알맞은 것을 고르시오 (1~20)

01 A temporary _____ of train service will cause delays of up to 25 minutes for commuters.

① irritation
③ controversy
② outbreak
④ disruption

02 It can be difficult to _____ to a new office environment when you do not know anyone there.

① assemble
③ adapt
② assign
④ affix

03 The two sides came to a _____ satisfactory solution after hammering out a deal overnight.

① separately
③ objectively
② arbitrarily
④ mutually

04 At Green Solutions, we _____ our customers to recycle in an effort to better protect the environment.

① seek
③ express
② urge
④ insist

05 Ace Enterprises has welcomed data from the federal government indicating continuing _____ with the nation's economic recovery.

① sensitivity
③ stability
② sustainability
④ disability

06 There has been an _____ rise in consumer spending this holiday season, leading to record profits for many stores.

① accomplished   ② abundant
③ informed   ④ unprecedented

07 Valerie is a big _____ of the project that Mr. Dalhousie proposed at the last meeting.

① advocate   ② reform
③ admission   ④ performance

08 Quite a lot of files were lost in the _____ of moving offices, leading to a serious problem.

① sensation   ② supposition
③ distinction   ④ confusion

09 Tyman and Four Stars are _____ the leading industrial waste management firms in the business.

① properly   ② respectively
③ positively   ④ confidentially

10 The offices of Gray and Smith will be closed on Monday in _____ of Memorial Day.

① allowance   ② observance
③ combination   ④ relation

11 Recently, a Malaysian company was _____ penalized by the WTO for unfair trade practices.

① sincerely   ② thoroughly
③ severely   ④ carefully

12 Please fill out every park of the following form, _____ the last section, and hand it to one of the clerks.

① enact   ② detach
③ assist   ④ demand

13 Most of the conference rooms remained _____ throughout the day even though several meetings had been scheduled.

① unprepared   ② undeveloped
③ unoccupied   ④ unemployed

14 Because of budget _____, employees are no longer offered free meals at lunch in the cafeteria.

① notations   ② constraints
③ inhibitions   ④ appreciations

15 _____ attendees at the conference will include the prime minister, the minister, the minister of finance, and our CEO.

① Exclusive   ② Feasible
③ Prominent   ④ Incessant

16 Customers have no _____to report to our sales staff, but they are encouraged to leave feedback.

① obligation   ② surplus
③ indication   ④ forecast

17 Skateboarders must attend an orientation meeting to learn about every safety _____ of the park.

① advice   ② rules   ③ idea   ④ precaution

18 In the coming years, the number of smartphone users will continue to rise
_____, increasing to 2 billion by 2018.

① previously   ② markedly
③ typically   ④ cordially

19 Be advised that baggage _____ cannot exceed 40kg, with a maximum of
two checked bags allowed at the counter.

① authorization   ② permission
③ material   ④ allowance

20 It's best to _____ of the company's confidential documents by shredding them
with the basement shredder.

① relieve   ② consist
③ dispose   ④ notify

[정답]

1	2	3	4	5	6	7	8	9	10
④	③	④	②	③	④	①	④	②	②
11	12	13	14	15	16	17	18	19	20
③	②	③	②	③	①	④	②	④	③

6. 어휘 예상 문제 (6회)

※ 다음 밑줄 친 부분에 들어갈 가장 알맞은 것을 고르시오. (1~20)

01 In a bid to _____ meager domestic sales, Calphalon Industries exported its products to six new countries overseas.

① supplement   ② impose
③ pursue   ④ add

02 Many people believe diesel engines are much more _____ than gasoline engines, but, in, fact, it depends on the vehicles.

① economical   ② industrial
③ unviable   ④ familiar

03 Results from the latest environmental studies are _____ with tests carried out in the past.

① continuous   ② consecutive
③ constant   ④ consistent

04 Although not a mandatory park of their contracts, HR is stressing that people _____ more time to volunteer activities.

① endow   ② provide
③ support   ④ devote

05 Seen from the reverse _____, the union members did not achieve nearly all of their goals.

① perspective   ② consideration
③ effect   ④ speculation

06 It is best if you _____ yourself with the machine's operation before attempting to use it.

① initiate   ② face
③ familiarize   ④ subordinate

07 In _____ with last year, productivity has not been as high because of a strike at one of our plants.

① charge   ② hesitation
③ comparison   ④ agreement

08 If the label information placed on a product is _____, it is important to contact a representative from that company at once.

① inaccurate   ② collective
③ abundant   ④ sequent

09 Keep in mind that the schedule is considered _____, so check back before the meeting starts to confirm any changes.

① vigilant   ② contemporary
③ infinite   ④ tentative

10 Shirley _____ requested that the order be sent by Monday, but it was sent out on Wednesday.

① relatively   ② fiercely
③ repeatedly   ④ respectively

11 _____ regulations dictate that every single item included in a package from another country be declared.

① Values   ② Customs
③ Refunds   ④ Expenses

12 The new factory is in the _____, of a neighborhood which is known for having many industrial sites.

① productivity   ② precaution
③ proximity   ④ promotion

13 Employees are required to take a _____ course being taught by the government on health and safety issues.

① mandatory   ② variable
③ careful   ④ unique

14 They expect the government to _____ the process of getting permits for construction projects.

① streamline   ② modernize
③ yield   ④ exert

15 If the bank does not _____ Ms. Kim for the mistake made with her wire transfer, she will file a formal complaint.

① give   ② send
③ succeed   ④ compensate

16 The senior vice president of media relations made an _____ decision once she was briefed by her aide.

① prepared   ② pictured
③ informed   ④ exposed

17 It's best to _____ yourself with the standard operating procedures at this firm as soon as you are hired.

① propose   ② acquaint   ③ practice   ④ employ

18 _____ grain from last year's harvest will be used by the government as donations to less developed nations.

① Lengthy   ② Opportune
③ Surplus   ④ Brief

19 I think it's best if we _____ our research to include emerging markets in Latin America and the Middle East.

① multiply   ② broaden
③ result   ④ impress

20 The company decided to open a new store in the heart of downtown as it is the mose _____ location.

① ongoing   ② reflected
③ pending   ④ strategic

[정답]

1	2	3	4	5	6	7	8	9	10
①	①	④	④	①	③	③	①	④	③

11	12	13	14	15	16	17	18	19	20
②	③	①	①	④	③	②	③	②	④

7. 어휘 예상 문제 (7회)

※ 다음 밑줄 친 부분에 들어갈 가장 알맞은 것을 고르시오. (1~20)

01 Dr. Maloney tried to _____ his talk in two minutes but ended up taking more than ten minutes.

① summarize   ② convince
③ delegate   ④ budget

02 When the crane stopped working at our New Delhi plant, it was a _____ unexpected breakdown.

① wealthy   ② valuable
③ mutual   ④ costly

03 This report includes the company's sales _____ for the next 12 quarters.

① disregard   ② projections
③ vacate   ④ ratings

04 At their last meeting, the R&D team decided to _____ on green technology advancements over the next five years.

① disregard   ② resign
③ vacate   ④ concentrate

05 One of my co-workers has received some excellent _____ from many of the more senior staff members.

① complements   ② compartments
③ compliments   ④ developments

06 Sheila paid a little more for _____ mileage with ger rental car because she was traveling a long distance.

① uncontrolled   ② unwarranted
③ unlimited   ④ unrecoverable

07 Mr. Wainwright asked security personnel to _____ enforce the new building regulations that pertain to all visitors.

① strictly   ② frankly
③ unduly   ④ nearly

08 When sending _____ items in the mail, you should take out insurance on the package.

① appropriate   ② durable
③ fragile   ④ spoiled

09 Our successes in workplace safety and health can be attributed to the _____ efforts of the entire staff.

① evidential   ② evaluative
③ deliberate   ④ changeable

10 Business expectations have been _____ in Ukraine ever since the election of the country's latest president.

① deteriorating   ② entailing
③ involving   ④ preparing

11 Although the _____ studies are complete, there have been no decisive conclusions.

① judicial   ② diligent
③ multilateral   ④ preliminary

12 We need to _____ the system if we are going to make it more effective.

① simplify   ② objectify
③ verbalize   ④ patronize

13 The personnel director was _____ negative in her critique of Larry's job performance over the last month.

① all   ② somewhat
③ some   ④ whatever

14 Many lending institutions announced they would be implementing hiring freezes in _____ years.

① next   ② followed
③ late   ④ subsequent

15 Please remember that the tour bus will be leaving from outside the museum's front entrance at _____ 10 A.M.

① happily   ② previously
③ precisely   ④ preventively

16 Porter deodorant is _____ priced and probably the most ecofriendly product of all deodorants.

① properly   ② absolutely
③ decidedly   ④ reasonably

17 Our department needs to _____ improve the way we communicate with other departments on technical matters.

① previously   ② initially   ③ gradually   ④ sparingly

18 I placed an _____, request with Marsha to expedite the item's delivery.

① automated   ② full
③ urgent   ④ rather

19 Anyone who wishes to take vacation time must first get _____ from Tom Evans, chief of the personnel division.

① condition   ② contraction
③ conclusion   ④ consent

20 Employees have been asked to review all pertinent regulations to ensure _____ with new government guidelines.

① compliance   ② observance
③ reference   ④ exception

[정답]

1	2	3	4	5	6	7	8	9	10
①	④	②	④	③	③	①	③	③	①
11	12	13	14	15	16	17	18	19	20
④	①	②	④	③	④	③	③	④	①

8. 어휘 예상 문제 (8회)

※ 다음 밑줄 친 부분에 들어갈 가장 알맞은 것을 고르시오. (1~20)

01 Mark is _____ the delivery of some paperwork from Mr. Gary Morgan, who applied for the vacancy in his department.

  ① submitting   ② ordering
  ③ relocating   ④ awaiting

02 Failure to work with Brian Jonestown on the _____ plan may result in termination or changes in position.

  ① attaching   ② attached
  ③ attachment   ④ attach

03 Building the factory here will be _____ to nearby residents as the company will be hiring more than 200 people.

  ① beneficial   ② additional
  ③ affordable   ④ capable

04 Y&T Ltd. makes a wide variety of _____ goods that come with a two-year warranty.

  ① durable   ② reversible
  ③ regular   ④ impeccable

05 When terminating an employee's contract, _____ must be given at least 15 years ahead of time for legal purposes.

  ① provision   ② notification
  ③ proposal   ④ communication

06 You can fill out the form _____ or on paper, whichever is more convenient for you.

① electronically   ② lately
③ exactly   ④ largely

07 Terry _____ his claim to the stock option so that there would no concerns about a breach of ethics.

① deleted   ② obtained
③ increased   ④ waived

08 Fasten the strap on your helmet _____ before entering the plant as objects have been known to fall from above.

① securely   ② vaguely
③ evenly   ④ anxiously

09 I have no _____ of taking any vacation time off this summer as things are just too hectic around the office.

① increase   ② error
③ effort   ④ intention

10 The IT employees had to _____ the program for employee use because people complained it was too complicated.

① excurse   ② train
③ customize   ④ build

11 There was a _____ drop in the price of rubber after Malaysia announced it was increasing its exports.

① live   ② dramatic
③ anxious   ④ confidential

12 In order to _____ deal with your concern, please indicate when and where you purchased our product.

① needlessly   ② accurately
③ eagerly   ④ totally

13 The workshop prepares its employees with real-life problem-solving skills, strong communication skills, and _____ research skills.

① conditional   ② unanimous
③ independent   ④ empty

14 A _____ outcome of the talks going on between the two companies will be an MOU.

① responsive   ② probable
③ capable   ④ likely

15 Ronald was _____ to do the work assigned to him because he didn't feel it was his responsibility.

① effective   ② dependent
③ inaudible   ④ reluctant

16 Ms. Darcy gave no _____ that she was in any way unsatisfied with her job at the company.

① obligation   ② surplus
③ indication   ④ forecast

17 The labor union has raised a number of _____ issues and plans on holding a strike if their demands aren't met.

① cost   ② wage   ③ salary   ④ charge

18 In _____ with the procedures laid out at the last safety meeting, visitors must wear a helmet and protective eyewear.

① charge

② accordance

③ approximation

④ collaboration

19 Anyone who does not _____ to the rules associated with workplace etiquette may be reprimanded by their superior.

① adhere

② comply

③ belong

④ access

20 We _____ interact with customers on behalf of our business partner.

① occasionally

② slightly

③ typically

④ decidedly

[정답]

1	2	3	4	5	6	7	8	9	10
④	②	①	①	②	①	④	①	④	③
11	12	13	14	15	16	17	18	19	20
②	②	③	②	④	③	②	②	①	①

9. 어휘 예상 문제 (9회)

※ 다음 밑줄 친 부분에 들어갈 가장 알맞은 것을 고르시오. (1~20)

01 If you visit us online, you will find a(n) _____ price list of every service that we offer.

① comprehensive ② eligible
③ professional ④ selective

02 Please note that you are _____ to a gift certificate because you ordered a combo pack special.

① asked ② invited
③ issued ④ entitled

03 The seminar was both _____ and interesting, and everyone was satisfied with it.

① respective ② informative
③ impressed ④ courteous

04 The two banks made _____ contributions to a number of charities, including Peace for Hope.

① substantial ② chronological
③ progressive ④ accessible

05 The two companies agreed to work _____ on the matter even though they signed an MOU on the research.

① variably ② separately
③ indirectly ④ presumably

06 You can _____ the service regulations as needed by phoning one of our representatives or by logging onto Web site.

① collate   ② comply
③ satisfy   ④ modify

07 They agreed to adopt a new set of _____ strategies on order to survive the upcoming recession.

① managerial   ② supervisory
③ marginal   ④ acceptable

08 With the _____ contribution by Timothy Pubark, we have been able to achieve our sales goals.

① exceptional   ② exclusive
③ expected   ④ experimental

09 The for ATMs are _____ located on the first floor fight beside the entrance.

① conveniently   ② consistently
③ heavily   ④ frequently

10 There was a temporary _____ of our security system in the past because of a software glitch.

① failure   ② arrival
③ complaint   ④ report

11 Researchers wanted to _____ with a new paint that would be weather resistant and cheap to make.

① endorse   ② experiment
③ justify   ④ ration

12 Please _____ your receipt in case the product is defective or not working and you need a full refund or exchange.

① sustain   ② assign

③ retain   ④ apply

13 At this point, it us unclear how _____ the Sales Department reaches its monthly sales target.

① conveniently   ② consistently

③ heavily   ④ vaguely

14 The _____ variation in fruit and vegetable consumption has been documented in quite a few studies.

① seasonal   ② objective

③ conscious   ④ respectful

15 Horrible weather conditions and technological malfunctions are _____ responsible for the delay in cleanup efforts.

① largely   ② diligently

③ initially   ④ adequately

16 Leadership training courses are held _____ for senior employees and upper management.

① exclusively   ② gradually

③ nearly   ④ precisely

17 Should you experience the _____ of your internet services, please contact the number at the bottom of this page.

① division   ② propositions   ③ interruption   ④ opportunity

18 The new inventory computer program in superior to the previous one in every _____ though it was quite expensive to install.

① assistance ② aspect
③ inclination ④ contention

19 Fuel cells are devices that _____ hydrogen gas into low-voltage, direct-current electricity.

① convert ② replace
③ design ④ produce

20 Two thousand copies of the annual sustainability report will be published at the end of this _____ year.

① marked ② due
③ ready ④ fiscal

[정답]

1	2	3	4	5	6	7	8	9	10
②	④	②	①	②	④	①	①	①	①
11	12	13	14	15	16	17	18	19	20
②	③	②	①	①	①	③	②	①	④

10. 어휘 예상 문제 (10회)

※ 다음 밑줄 친 부분에 들어갈 가장 알맞은 것을 고르시오. (1~20)

01 This _____ can be used at any of our lodges or spas from now until December 31, 2018.

① violation   ② validity
③ volume   ④ voucher

02 As a three-time _____ of the Best Employee of the Year award, Thomas Vokoon was considered qualified for the position.

① occupant   ② replacement
③ recipient   ④ renovation

03 The las firm has adopted a _____ working schedule, which has made it popular with job applicants.

① versatile   ② flexible
③ vulnerable   ④ hesitant

04 There are many things to do at the Blumberry Department Store _____ shopping.

① whether   ② neither
③ unless   ④ besides

05 While the _____ tasks associated with this job might seem mundane, they are very important.

① routine   ② rival
③ conclusive   ④ exhausted

06 At the end of the team meeting, he briefly _____ on Mandy Chelsea's transfer to New York.

① developed   ② proceeded
③ remarked   ④ persuaded

07 Anyone who does not _____ with the company's regulations will be asked to leave the factory.

① confirm   ② comply
③ remind   ④ agree

08 Hall and Oates is _____ of becoming a major player among Vancouver law firms.

① significant   ② able
③ capable   ④ essential

09 In order to _____ all of our goals, we are going to need to hire 10 more people.

① enlarge   ② communicate
③ declare   ④ accomplish

10 Rubber production has _____ increased over the last two years, driving down prices worldwide.

① accidentally   ② always
③ slightly   ④ naturally

11 To _____ unnecessary risks in everyday operations, we have made strong corporate governance a top priority.

① forward   ② exchange
③ eliminate   ④ lavish

12 The cellular phone business has become a very _____ industry for a number of companies.

① partial   ② consecutive
③ fluent   ④ profitable

13 If the partner company does not cease and desist, we will be forced to take
action _____.

① gradually   ② absolutely
③ potentially   ④ accordingly

14 You will have to pardon the _____ of the office a as it is currently
undergoing renovations.

① appearance   ② tournament
③ strength   ④ arbitration

15 Mrs. Fontana has been _____ to ensuring that API is recognized globally
as an employer.

① increased   ② recommended
③ dedicated   ④ agreed

16 The _____ pace of sales has helped fuel the strongest quarter in profits
for the manufacturing sector.

① pleased   ② convenient
③ steady   ④ creative

17 It looks like weather conditions will be _____ for Saturday's annual staff
sports day event.

① favorable   ② satisfied   ③ enlightening   ④ sudden

18 The _____ necessary to trade stocks legally is one which can only be
obtained through the FCC.

① certification   ② conclusion
③ attempts   ④ appropriation

19 The _____ industry has seen a serious decline in the number of tourists coming to visit the city.

① cultivation   ② altruism
③ fondness   ④ hospitality

20 High unemployment across the country is a major _____ in the government's implementing a spending initiative.

① oversight   ② decision
③ similarity   ④ factor

[정답]

1	2	3	4	5	6	7	8	9	10
④	③	②	④	①	③	②	③	④	③
11	12	13	14	15	16	17	18	19	20
③	④	④	①	③	③	①	①	④	④

Part 3 ··· 토익 독해

◆ 1. 독해의 기본 요령

1. 독해 순서

① 주절 동사 찾기	- 문장의 핵심은 동사이므로 주절의 동사를 찾는다. - 동사와 연관된 문법은 시제, 조동사, 태, 일치이다.
② 수식어 찾기	- 문장의 주어, 목적어, 보어로 사용되는 명사는 앞 뒤에서 형용사에 의해 수식을 받는다. (한정사) (형용사)명사(형용사구:전치사구,분사구,부정사) (관계절) - 동사는 부사에 의해 수식을 받는다. (부사)동사(부사구:전치사구) (부사절:때, 이유, 양보, 조건, 목적)
③ 문장 5형식 확인	- 수식어를 찾아 괄호를 치면 남는 단어가 문장 5형식의 주요소가 되어 형식을 확인할 수 있다.

2. 독해 방법

① 저자의 의도(요지) 파악	- 독해지문은 저자가 어떤 목적을 가지고 쓰기 때문에 저자의 의도를 파악하는 것이 중요하다. - 저자의 의도는 지문 첫 문장이나 첫 단락에 주로 나타나므로 처음 부분을 읽고 요지와 주제를 파악해야 한다.
② 단어 중심이 아닌 의미 중심	- 문장은 주제에 맞게 통일성을 가지고 쓰여 지므로 모르는 단어에 너무 집착하지 말고 문맥 중심으로 해석해야 한다.
③ 속독	- 시간부족으로 문제를 다 풀지 못하는 경우가 많으므로 문장 처음을 보고 요지 파악 후 예문을 읽고 정답을 찾는다.

독해 예문 (수식어 찾는 연습)

① The **parliament** of Australia's Northern Territory **passed** the world's first **law** that permits medically assisted voluntary euthanasia. (3형식)

(호주 북부 주의 의회가 의학적으로 도움이 되는 자발적인 안락사를 허용하는 세계 최초의 법을 통과시켰다.)

② His **father** who had been a great general of the armies of Athens **died** when the boy was very young. (1형식)

(아테네 군대의 위대한 장군이었던 그의 아빠는 소년이 매우 어렸을 때 죽었다.)

③ **Hospices treat patients** suffering from incurable diseases who are not expected to live for more than a year. (3형식)   (호스피스들은 일 년 이상 살 것으로 기대되지 않는 불치병으로 고통 받는 환자들을 돌본다.)

④ **What** he said **was lost** in the applause that greeted him. (2형식)

(그가 한 말은 그를 환영하는 환호성에 파 묻혔다.)

⑤ The **law** (that) I am referring to **requires that everyone who owns a car have accident insurance.** (3형식)

(내가 가리키는 그 법은 차를 소유한 모든 사람들이 사고보험에 들것을 요구하고 있다.)

⑥ **Businessmen advertize** to make us feel like buying what they sell. (1형식)

(사업가들은 그들이 팔고자 하는 물건을 우리로 하여금 사고 싶은 마음이 들게 하려고 광고한다.)

⑦ The **reason** (why) grass is green **was** a **mystery** to the child. (2형식)

(잔디가 푸르른 이유는 어린아이에게는 신비한 일이다.)

⑧ **This is** the same **watch** as I lost yesterday. (2형식)

(이것이 내가 어제 잃어버린 것과 똑 같은 시계이다.)

⑨ There **is** also **evidence** that physical activity decreases with age. (1형식)

(신체적인 활동이 나이를 먹어감에 따라 쇠퇴하는 증거가 역시 있다.)

⑩ The poor **cows** working hard to furrow the stony soil of the wide farm in the daytime **give** abundantly with no complaint the **men** of the farm fresh nourishing **milk** in the morning. (4형식)

(대낮에 넓은 농장의 돌이 많은 땅을 경작하기 위해 열심히 일하는 불쌍한 소들은 아무 불평 없이 농장의 일꾼에게 아침에 신선하고 영양분이 많은 우유를 풍부하게 제공한다.)

◆ 2. 토익 독해 문제 [PART 6]

[PART 6]

Directions: Read the texts that follow. A word, phrase, or sentence is missing in parts of each text. Four answer choices for each question are given below the text. Select the best answer to complete the text. Then mark the ①, ②, ③, or④ on your answer sheet.

[1-4] refer to the following article.

Mountain Heights Travel News

By Leela Roberts

SPRINGFEILD (10 September)-On 4 September, Flying Star Airways __(1)__ its new, individualized baggage-tracking application. Industry analyst Simon Kneppers calls it "one of Flying Star's most innovative ideas yet." The new system is simple: When the bags arrive, passengers are alerted by online notification to the specific baggage-claim area where they are located. __(2)__, the application notifies passengers when there are delays. __(3)__. Passengers can choose to have notifications __(4)__ by text message or e-mail. The free app is available for download on most smartphones.

01 ① canceled   ② reported   ③ launched   ④ examined

02 ① Instead   ② Eventually   ③ In addition   ④ As a result

03 ① Passengers were notified of their seat assignments.
② The system will even notify passengers if their bags will arrive on a later flight.
③ Passengers are advised to make their bags easily distinguishable.
④ Baggage-claim carousels have been upgraded.

04 ① deliver　② delivered　③ are delivering　④ to deliver

[5-8] refer to the following regulations.

Packaging and Transferring Flammable Liquids

All vehicles and containers that transport flammable liquids must be clearly identified. Specific requirements for the ___(5)___ can be found on page 6 of this document.

　As a general rule, red diamond-shaped stickers with white text should be used. Please note that details may vary from region to region. If you are ___(6)___ of the exact requirements for your area, always contact the National Transportation Bureau directly.

　While the sender must supply the correct stickers for each container ___(7)___, it is the carrier's responsibility to make sure they are properly affixed to the containers. Vehicles carrying flammable liquids must also display a placard that is readily visible to other drivers. ___(8)___.

---

05 ① labels　② studies　③ catalogs　④ transactions

06 ① unheard　② unsure　③ independent　④ incapable

07 ① transports　② transporting
　　③ being transported　④ having been transported

08 ① There are several possibilities for parking.
　　② It has been placed there for your convenience.
　　③ This is an option when the loading area is occupied.
　　④ No exceptions are to be made under any circumstances.

[9-12] refer to the following announcement.

Nyveg Technology Hardware Competition

Nyveg Ventures is now accepting applications for our sixth annual Technology Hardware Competition to be held in Oslo, Norway, beginning on 1 November. We will be selecting teams from around the world who have taken new hardware projects past the idea stage and have already built a working prototype.

___(9)___. Accepted applicants will spend one week in Oslo working on further developing ___(10)___ prototypes. Each of the accepted teams will receive funding and technical support from our partners. ___(11)___, Nyveg Ventures' experienced business mentors will provide intensive education and practical guidance on marketing. Nyveg Ventures' ___(12)___ for the competition is to support the development of promising new hardware products as they go to market.

---

09 ① Applications should be submitted online by 15 September.
② Nyveg maintains three separate offices throughout Europe.
③ Universities in Norway offer many quality programs in technology.
④ Late applications have been returned by the review committee.

10 ① they ② them ③ their ④ theirs

11 ① Otherwise ② Therefore ③ Nevertheless ④ Moreover

12 ① purposeful ② purpose ③ purposes ④ purposely

[13~16] refer to the following letter.

Hopingvill Garden and Flower Society

P.O. Bos 2331

Ontario, Canada L5A 2J2

10 February

Dear Mr. Garcia,

The Garden and Flower Society is proud to announce that we   (13)   our fifth Spring Garden and Houseplant Sale on Saturday, 3 May.   (14)   . It is scheduled to coincide with the annual downtown Spring Fling shopping day. As usual, we will have vendors selling homemade soups and breads, unique garden ornaments, and artwork. Since you sold your   (15)   watercolor paintings at last year's sale, I thought you might want to join us again this year. I am attaching the necessary information and application form if you are interested in   (16)   . we look foreword to hearing from you.

Sincerely,

Sanford Sladen

GFS Events Coordinator

---

13 ① hold   ② held   ③ holding   ④ will hold

14 ① I am the events coordinator for the Garden and Flower Society.

② Thank you for helping to make this event a spectacular success.

③ This event takes place every year on the front lawn at the Forest Park.

④ Please excuse our appearance as we begin to replant our garden.

15 ① lengthy   ② lovely   ③ confident   ④ youthful

16 ① purchasing   ② touring   ③ interviewing   ④ participating

◆ 3. 토익 독해 문제 [PART 7]

[PART 7]

Directions: In this part you will read a selection of texts, such as magazine and newspaper articles, e-mails, and instant messages. Each text or set of texts is followed by several questions. Select the best answer to complete the text. Then mark the ①, ②, ③, or④ on your answer sheet.

[17-18] refer to the following policy.

Maxima Emporium-Return Policy

In order to be eligible for return or exchange, articles must not show evidence of having been worn,, washed, or damaged, and original tags must be attached. Refunds are only possible if the item is returned within 30 days of purchase and is accompanied by the original sales receipt. If returning an online purchase, you may show the digital receipt on your mobile device. If the 30-day period has expired or you do not have a receipt, you may return the item for store credit, which can be applied toward a future purchase. An article may be exchange without a receipt for the same product in a different size or color.

17 What type of products does Maxima Emporiym sell?

① Clothing ② Cleaning supplies ③ Computers ④ Mobile phones

18 Why must customers present a sales receipt?

① To avoid paying a fee   ② To exchange a product
③ To make a return after 30 days   ④ To receive a refund

[19-20] refer to the following page from an instructional guide.

Anand Creek Lodge

Anand Creek Lodge is committed to maintaining a high level of cleanliness and guest satisfaction. By following the cleaning and maintenance procedures outlined in this guide, you can help us uphold these standards.

In the following pages, you will learn about loading the trolley with fresh sheets, towels, and supplies; respectfully entering and cleaning the guest rooms; and servicing the lobby, dining room, and other public areas.

Once you have finished reading, go to www.anandcreeklodge.com/form99 and answer the questions about the procedures and practices covered in the guide. This form must be completed by the end of your first week of employment.

---

19 For whom are the instructions intended?

① Hotel guests   ② Cleaning staff

③ Restaurant serves   ④ Employee trainers

20 Why would someone complete the online questionnaire?

① To apply for a job opening

② To document a maintenance problem

③ To demonstrate that procedures are understood

④ To suggest ways to improve processes

[21-24] refer to the following article.

About Town

SYNDNEY (15 Feb.) — Following the success of her dinner-kit company in the United Kingdom, Marissa Arnold has launched an Australian version of Fresh from Marissa. A growing trend in many cities, meal-kit delivery services offer all the ingredients needed for a meal that subscribers then cook for themselves. They are viewed as a cost-effective alternative to eating in restaurants or alternative to eating in restaurants or buying takeaway food. The meals can be cooked at home without the fuss of shopping for food or finding new recipes.

One might say Ms. Arnold has repackaged herself more than once. She began her professional career as a college professor. Then she gave it up, traveled to Tuscany, and attended a cooking school. After her time in Tuscany, she opened a restaurant in Edinburgh, which she sold four years ago. She has since gained fame with a television show based in Edinburgh, which airs here as well.

Fresh from Marissa's meal-kit delivery service launched last week in Sydney, where Ms. Arnold will soon promote the new product. She will give a demonstration at the Parcy Market on Bridge Street on Saturday, 25 February, at 1:00 P.M. In May, Fresh from Marissa will launch in Brisbane. If all goes well, the service should be available in other Australian cities, including Melbourne and Perth, by the end of the year.

---

21 What is indicated about Fresh from Marissa?

① It is available in different countries.

② It was founded in Tuscany.

③ It was inspired by a television show.

④ It delivers freshly cooked meals.

22 What is mentioned as a benefit of the meal kits?

① They are tailored to fit unique dietary requirements.

② They include a shopping list of necessary ingredients.

③ They are less expensive than many restaurant meals.

④ They are precooked in order to save time in the kitchen.

23 What was Ms. Arnold's first career?

① Travel agent   ② Educator   ③ Chef   ④ Restaurant owner

24 Where will Ms. Arnold be on February 25?

① In Edinburgh   ② In Sydney   ③ In Brisbane   ④ In Melbourne

[25-28] refer to the following e-mail.

E-Mail Message
To: c_gonzalez@uniflicks.com
From: bachmant@coremetrica.com
Date: October 26
Subject: Web site analysis
Attachment: Uniflicks data

Dear Ms. Gonzales

As you requested, I performed an evaluation of your Web site, uniflicks.com, resulting in the following preliminary conclusion.

Your articles about the film industry and film industry professionals, while well-written and informative, include too many graphics or pictures. As a result, text is broken up into awkward segments, forcing visitors to the site to scroll down so frequently that they lose interest in the piece they are reading. Specifically, they often leave a page after having read just half of an article. Even worse, many abandon the site altogether. having spent no more than five minutes browsing through it. Please see the attached chart for more specifics related to this matter.

One solution to the problem might be to use photographs and graphics sparingly, preferably limited to those that are particularly eye-catching.

If you would like me to conduct a more in-depth analysis, I would be happy to do so. Dataluge, the software I used to evaluate your site, is able to determine which words users type into search engines to find your Web site. Such a report will provide you with ideas for modifying your site so that you can better attract and retain visitors.

Best regards,

Tobias Bachman
Coremetrica, Inc.

25 The word "performed" in paragraph 1, line 1, is closest in meaning to

① operated   ② relied on   ③ carried out   ④ entertained

26 According to the e-mail, what is the problem with the images on the Web site?

① They are too small.   ② They are of low quality.
③ They make the text hard to read. ④ They are not related to the articles.

27 What does the attachment show?

① How many Web sites about the film industry there are
② What images are most popular on the Internet
③ What words users enter into search engines
④ How much time visitors spend reading articles on the Web site

28 What does Mr. Bachman offer to do?

① Evaluate the Web site further   ② Suggest new topics for articles

③ Implement the necessary changes   ④ Show how to use a software program

[토익 독해 정답]

1	2	3	4	5	6	7	8	9	10
③	③	②	②	①	②	③	④	①	③
11	12	13	14	15	16	17	18	19	20
④	②	④	③	②	④	①	④	②	③
21	22	23	24	25	26	27	28		
①	③	②	②	③	③	④	①		

[토익 독해 해설]

마운틴 하이츠 교통 정보

[1-4] (해석)

글 릴라 로버츠

스프링필드(9월 10일)—9월 4일 플라잉 스타 항공은 새로운 개별 수하물 추적 애플리케이션을 출시했다. 기업 분석가 사이먼 네퍼스는 이 프로그램을 "플라잉 스타의 가장 혁신적인 아이디어 중 하나"라고 부른다.

새로운 시스템은 간단하다. 짐이 도착하면 승객은 짐이 있는 특정 수화물 찾는 곳을 온라인으로 통보 받는다. 뿐만 아니라, 이 애플리케이션은 지연이 발생하면 승객에게 알려준다. 심지어 이 시스템은 짐이 더 늦은 비행편으로 도착할 경우 승객에게 알려줄 것이다. 승객들은 문자 메시지 또는 이메일로 통보가 전송되도록 선택할 수 있다. 이 무료 앱은 대다수 스마트폰에서 다운로드할 수 있다.

[어휘] launch: 출시하다, 출범하다 individualize: 개인 요구에 맞추다 baggage: 수하물, 짐, 가방 analyst: 분석가 innovate: 혁신적인 yet: 지금까지 passenger: 승객 alert: 경보를 발하다 notification: 통보 specific: 특정한, 구체적인 claim: 주장하다, (자신의 재산이라고) 요구하다 in addition: 게다가 notify: 통보하다 delay: 지연, 지체 flight: 항공편 deliver: 배달하다, 전달하다 available: 이용 가능한

[5-8] (해석)

인화성 액체 포장 및 운송

인화성 액체를 운송하는 모든 차량과 컨테이너는 명확하게 식별되어야 합니다. 라벨의 구체적인 요건을 이 문서의 6페이지에서 확인할 수 있습니다.

일반적으로 적색의 다이아몬드 모양 스티커에 백색 글자를 사용해야 합니다. 세부사항은 지역에 따라 다를 수 있다는 점을 유의하십시오. 본인 지역의 정확한 요건을 확실히

알지 못한다면, 항상 미국 교통국에 직접 연락하십시오.

발송자는 운송되는 각 컨테이너에 맞는 스티커를 제공해야 하지만, 스티커를 적절하게 컨테이너에 부착하는 것은 책임입니다. 인화선 액체를 운반하는 차량에는 다른 운전자가 쉽게 볼 수 있는 플래카드도 부착해야 합니다. 어떤 경우에도 예외는 없습니다.

[어휘] package: 포장하다 transfer: 이동하다, 운반하다 flammable: 인화성의 liquid: 액체 vehicle: 차량 transport: 운송하다 identify: 식별하다 specific: 구체적인, 특정한 requirement: 요건, 요구 사항 as a general rule: 대개는 vary: 다르다 region: 지역 unsure: 확신이 없는 contact: 연락하다 transportation: 교통, 운송 bureau (관청의) 부서, 국 directly: 직접, 바로 supply: 제공하다 responsibility: 책임 properly: 적절하게 affix: 부착하다 placard: 플래카드, 현수막 visible: 보이는, 알아볼 수 있는 under any circumstances: 어떠한 경우에도

[9-12]　(해석)

나이백 테크놀로지 하드웨어 경연 대회

나이백 벤처스는 11월 1일부터 노르웨이 오슬로에서 열리는 제 6회 연례 테크놀로지 하드웨어 경연 대회 참가 신청을 받고 있습니다. 우리는 전 세계에서 아이디어 단계를 넘어 새로운 하드웨어 프로젝트를 수행하고 또한 작동하는 시제품을 이미 제작한 팀을 선정할 것입니다. 신청서는 9월 15일까지 온라인으로 제출해야 합니다. 합격한 신청자는 오슬로에서 1주일을 체류하면서 시제품을 더 발전시키는 작업을 하게 됩니다. 합격한 팀은 모두 당시의 협력 업체로부터 자금 및 기술 지원을 받게 됩니다. 더욱이 나이백 벤처스의 노련한 경영 멘토들이 마케팅에 대한 집중적인 교육과 실용적인 지침을 제공할 예정입니다. 나이백 벤처스가 경연 대회를 여는 목적은 시장에 출시될 유망한 신제품 하드웨어의 개발을 지원하는 것입니다.

[어휘] competition: 경쟁, 경연 대회 accept: 받아들이다 application: 지원(서) annual: 해마다 일어나는, 연례의 prototype: 시제품, 원형 submit: 제출하다 applicant:

지원자 receive: 받다 funding: 자금[재정], 자금 지원 support: 지원; 지원하다 moreover: 게다가, 더욱이 experienced: 노련한, 경험이 많은 intensive: 집중적인 practical: 실용적인, 현실적인 guidance: 지도, 지침 purpose: 목적 development: 발전, 개발 promising: 유망한, 장래가 촉망되는

[13-16] (해석)
호핑빌 정원 및 꽃 협회
사서함 2331
온타리오, 캐나다 L5A2J2
2월 10일

가르시아 씨께,

정원 및 꽃 협회는 5월 3일 토요일에 제5회 봄 정원 및 실내용 화초 세일 판매 개최를 발표하게 되어 자랑스럽습니다. 이 행사는 매년 포레스트 공원 앞 잔디밭에서 열립니다. 해마다 도심에서 열리는 봄맞이 쇼핑일과 겹치도록 일정이 잡힙니다. 여느 때처럼 집에서 만든 수프와 빵, 독특한 정원 장식, 그리고 예술품을 판매하는 노점이 설 예정입니다. 귀하께서는 작년 세일 때 아름다운 수채화를 판매하셨기 때문에 올해도 함께 하셨으면 합니다. 참여 의사가 있으시다면 필요한 자료와 신청서를 첨부합니다. 연락 기다리겠습니다.

샌포드 슬레이든
GFS 행사 코디네이터

[어휘] proud: 자랑스러운 announce: 발표하다 houseplant: 실내용 화초, 화분 식물 take place: 일어나다, 발생하다 lawn: 잔디 coincide with: ~와 일치하다, 동시에 일어나다 annual: 해마다 일어나는, 연례의 as usual: 여느 때처럼, 평소처럼 vendor: 노점상, 판매상 unique: 독특한 ornament: 장식품 attach: 첨부하다 necessary: 필요한 application: 지원(서) participate: 참석하다 look forward to –ing: ~을 바라다, 기대하다 coordinator: 코디네이터, 진행자

[17-18] (해석)

맥시마 상점—반품 규정

반품이나 교환이 가능하려면 물품에 착용, 세탁, 또는 손상의 흔적이 없어야 하며, 반드시 원래의 꼬리표가 부착되어야 합니다. 환불은 물품이 구매일로부터 30일 이내에 반품이 이루어지고 판매 영수증 원본이 함께 제시되는 경우에만 가능합니다. 온라인 구매품을 반품하는 경우 모바일 장치의 디지털 영수증을 제시할 수 있습니다. 30일이 경과되었거나 영수증이 없는 경우에는 매장 포인트로 받는 조건으로 물품을 반품하실 수 있으며, 이는 향후 구매 시 적용될 수 있습니다. 교환은 영수증 없이 동일한 제품을 다른 크기나 색상으로 교환할 수 있습니다.

[어휘] emporium: 대형 상점 policy: 규정, 방침 be eligible for: ~할 자격이 되다 exchange: 교환; 교환하다 article: 물품 evidence: 증거, 흔적 wear: 입다, 착용하다 damage: 손상을 입히다 attach: 부착하다, 첨부하다: refund 환불(금) purchase: 구매(품); 구매하다 accompany: 동반하다 receipt: 영수증 device: 기기

[19-20] (해석)

아난드 계곡 산장

아난드 계곡 산장은 높은 수준의 청결과 고객 만족을 유지하기 위해 전력을 다하고 있습니다. 지침서에 설명된 청소 및 유지 관리 절차를 준수하면 이러한 수준을 유지하는 데 도움이 됩니다.
다음 페이지에서 카트에 새 시트, 수건 및 비품을 쌓는 방법, 객실에 정중히 들어가서 청소하는 방법, 로비, 식당, 그리고 기타 공공 장소에서 서비스하는 방법에 대해 알아봅니다.

다 읽으셨다면 www.anandcreeklodge.com/from99로 가서 지침서에 포함된 절차 및 관행에 대한 질문에 답하십시오. 본 양식은 근무 시작 후 첫 번째 주말까지 완료되어야 합니다.

[어휘] lodge: 오두막, 산장 be committed to: ~에 전념하다 cleanliness: 청결 satisfaction: 만족 maintenance :유지 관리, 정비 procedure: 절차 uphold: 유지하다 load: (짐 등을) 싣다 trolley: 카트 supplies: 비품, 저장품 respectfully: 정중하게, 공손하게 practice: 관행 cover: 다루다, 포함하다

[21-24] (해석)

시 소식

시드니(2월 15일)—마리사 아놀드는 영국에서 쿠킹 박스 회사로 성공을 거둔 후 호주에서 프레시 프롬 마리사를 출범했다. 많은 도시에서 증가하고 있는 추세인 쿠킹 박스 배달 서비스는 가입자들이 직접 요리해 먹을 수 있도록 필요한 모든 재료를 제공한다. 이 서비스는 식당에서 먹거나 테이크아웃 음식을 사는 것보다 저렴한 대안으로 인식되고 있다. 음식을 사러 가거나 새로운 요리법을 찾느라 법석을 떨지 않고도 집에서 요리할 수 있다.

아놀드 씨가 여러 번 변신했다고 말할 사람도 있을 것이다. 그녀는 대학 교수로 직업 경력을 쌓기 시작했다. 그런 다음에는 교수직을 포기하고 토스카나로 가서 요리학교에 다녔다. 토스카나에서 지낸 후, 그녀는 에든버러에서 식당을 열었고, 4년 전에 그것을 매각했다. 이후 그녀는 에든버러에서 방송되는 텔레비전 쇼로 유명해졌는데 이 쇼는 이곳에서도 방영된다.
프레시 프롬 마리사의 쿠킹 박스 배달 서비스가 지난주 시드니에서 시작되었으며, 아놀드 씨는 곧 그곳에서 신제품을 홍보할 예정이다. 그녀는 2월 25일 토요일 오후 1시에 브리지 가 파시 시장에서 제품 시연에 나선다. 프레시 프롬 마리사는 5월에 브리즈번에서 출범할 예정이다. 모든 일이 순조롭게 진행된다면 올해 말까지 멜버른, 퍼스를 포함한 다른 호주 도시들에서도 이 서비스를 이용할 수 있게 된다.

[어휘] dinner-kit: (요리 재료가 정량으로 담긴)쿠킹 박스 launch: 출시하다, 출범하다 growing: 커지는, 성장하는 meal-kit: 쿠킹 박스 delivery 배송, 배달 ingredient: 재료 subscriber: 구독자, 가입자 cost-effective: 비용 효율적인, 저렴한 alternative: 대안 takeaway: 테이크아웃 fuss 소란, 불편함 receipt: 요리법, 레시피 give up: 포기하다 attend: 다니다, 출석하다 gain: 얻다 fame: 명성, 유명세 air: 방송하다 promote: 홍보하다 demonstration: 시연

[25-28] （해석）
수신: c_gonzalez@uniflicks.com
발신: bachmant@coremetrica.com
날짜: 10월 26일
첨부: Uniflicks 자료

곤잘레스 씨께,

요청하신 대로, 저는 귀사의 웹사이트 uniflicks.com에 대한 평가를 수행했고, 다음과 같은 임시 결론을 내렸습니다.

영화 산업과 영화 산업 전문가들에 귀사의 기사들은 잘 쓰여졌으며 유익하지만 그래픽이나 사진이 너무 많습니다. 결과적으로 텍스트가 어색하게 분할되어, 방문자들로 하여금 너무 자주 스크롤을 내리게 하므로 그들이 읽고 있던 기사에 대한 흥미를 잃게 됩니다. 특히 방문자들은 종종 기사의 절반만 읽고 페이지를 벗어납니다. 더 심각한 문제는 많은 사람이 5분 정도만 둘러보고 사이트를 완전히 떠난다는 점입니다. 이 문제와 관련된 세부 내용은 첨부 도표를 참고하십시오.
이 문제에 대한 한 가지 해결책은 사진과 그래픽을 적게 사용하는 것으로, 가급적 특별히 눈길을 끄는 것으로만 제한하는 것이 좋습니다.
좀 더 면밀한 분석을 원하시면 기꺼이 해 드리겠습니다. 제가 귀사 사이트를 평가하기 위해 사용했던 소프트웨어인 데이터루지는 사용자가 귀사의 웹사이트를 찾을 때 검색 엔진에 어떤 단어를 입력하는지 알아낼 수 있습니다. 그런 보고서는 방문자를 더 많이 유치하고 머무를 수 있도록 귀사의 사이트를 수정하는데 필요한 아이디어를 제공할 것

입니다.

토비어스 바크만
코어메트리카사

[어휘] request: 요청하다 perform: 수행하다, 연주하다 evaluate: 평가 result in: 결과로
~이 되다 preliminary: 임시의, 예비의 conclusion: 결론 article: 기사, 논문
professional: 전문가 informative: 유익한 as a result: 그 결과, 따라서 break up:
부서지다, 깨지다 awkward: 보기 흉한 segment: 단편, 조각 force: 강요하다
frequently: 자주 specifically: 특히 abandon: 버리다 browse: 둘러보다, 훑어보다
attached: 첨부된 specifics: 세부 내용 related to: ~와 관련된 solution: 해결책
sparingly: 절약하여, 드물게 preferably: 가급적 particularly: 특히 eye-catching:
눈길을 끄는 conduct: 수행하다 in-depth: 심도 있는 analysis: 분석 evaluate: 평
가하다 determine: 판단하다, 결정하다 provide A with B: A에게 A를 제공하다
modify: 수정하다, 바꾸다 attract: 유인하다, 끌어들이다, retain: 붙잡아 두다

Part 4 ⋯ 토익 실전문제(100문제)

◆ 토익 실전 문제 (100문제)

01 Mr. Santos had to book the transportation _____ ecause of a last-minute change of plans.

① his own   ② himself   ③ his   ④ him

02 Applications for the accounting position must be received no _____ than April 19.

① later   ② after   ③ behind   ④ further

03 In order to _____ more tourists, the Henly Museum is offering free admission in July.

① attraction   ② attracting   ③ attractive   ④ attract

04 The cost of a train ticket is set to increase _____ on January 1.

① quickly   ② slightly   ③ urgently   ④ equally

05 In _____ for her years of service, the company threw Mrs. Parida a retirement party.

① appreciating   ② appreciative   ③ appreciate   ④ appreciation

06 This mapping application _____ tracks the user's position to determine the fastest route.

① automation   ② automatic   ③ automate   ④ automatically

07 Items that are returned incur a minimal restocking fee, to be deducted _____ your refund.

① from   ② below   ③ past   ④ upon

08 The agreement becomes _____ once both parties have signed the documents.

① effectively   ② effective   ③ effects   ④ effect

09 Chef Alice Grissom says she must decide _____ to open an additional restaurant in Strasbourg or to remain only in Colmar.

① for   ② it   ③ whether   ④ over

10 Sheffield Cinema _____ on presenting the best in foreign and independent movies.

① appear   ② refers   ③ occur   ④ focuses

11 Only _____ present at the board of directors meeting may vote on the issue.

① this   ② those   ③ whoever   ④ who

12 The engineering division is in the _____ of reviewing specifications for single-engine aircraft parts.

① plan   ② interest   ③ process   ④ custom

13 Ms. Rabanal has a great deal of experience with corporate taxation, _____ of it at the local level.

① many   ② few   ③ much   ④ any

14 _____ predictions by financial forecasters, Olmer Fuel Corporation's overall sales rose by 10 percent.

① Although   ② However   ③ Otherwise   ④ Despite

15 _____ employment contracts will be distributed at the end of the month.

① Revising   ② Revision   ③ Revised   ④ Revise

16 Companies often _____ with their contractors to find solutions to shared concerns.

① collaborate   ② evaluate   ③ conduct   ④ support

17 Ms. Allukian _____ produces high-quality work.

① consistently   ② consistency   ③ consistent   ④ consists

18 Mr. Tsai's tour sales last month were far _____ what had been anticipated.

① along   ② besides   ③ considering   ④ beyond

19 An _____ visitor to Semanteca Industries will notice many employees standing while working at their computers.

① observation   ② observable   ③ observant   ④ observed

20 Naju International's _____ of Asan Solutions caused Naju's stock prices to soar yesterday.

① drawback   ② acquisition   ③ provision   ④ indicator

21 Purchase receipts will now _____ electronically and sent to customers by e-mail.

① be generate   ② generating

③ have generating   ④ had been generating

22 _____ seafood processors have cleaned the fish, they package it for sale.

① Because   ② Once   ③ Much like   ④ Even as

23 You may adjust the _____ of your monitor so the image on the screen is suitable for viewing.

① brightness   ② brighter   ③ brighten   ④ bright

24 Because Dr, Yamato has already announced his departure, it is _____ that the board soon name a successor.

① sincere   ② equivalent   ③ imperative   ④ theoretical

25 Since the number of staff in our office will soon _____, we may need to install additional printing stations.

① double   ② bigger   ③ more   ④ increased

26 The photographs are displayed _____ to reflect society's progression over the years.

① extremely   ② chronologically   ③ biologically   ④ actually

27 Mr. Melniczak _____ the minutes of this afternoon's client meeting before the end of the day.

① distribute   ② to be distributed
③ will distribute   ④ has been distributing

28 Tourism has flourished in South Joree _____ the world has learned more about its beautiful beaches.

① still   ② as   ③ rather   ④ than

29 Tibb CEO Jung Park said he hopes his company can continue producing refrigerators _____ for the foreseeable future.

① sustainably   ② is sustained
③ sustaining   ④ sustain

30 It is fortunate that ms. Merritt's visit to Seattle _____ with the annual Small Business Expo.

① accesses   ② confirms   ③ accepts   ④ coincides

[Questions 31-34] refer to the following memo.

To : AI staff

From : Leo Guillen

___31___ to feedback from employees, the management team has decided   to change the procedure for using vacation leave.

Previously, at least two weeks' notice was required for taking time off, and   vacation requests were rejected on many occasions as a result of this strict rule. Under the new ___32___, employees are free to use their vacation days at any time, as long as the absence is approved by manager in advance.

___33___ Just be sure to make the necessary arrangements with you team.   Further details will be given at the ___34___ meeting. We hope you will   all benefit from the change.

31 ① Respond   ② Responds   ③ Responded   ④ Responding

32 ① policy   ② analysis   ③ factor   ④ symptom

33 ① Likewise, some departments have more problems with staff shortage than others.

   ② Specifically, the vacation schedule will be posted weekly in the break room.

   ③ Therefore, if you need to be absent on short notice, it is now acceptable.

   ④ From now on, the management team members will discuss the issue as a group.

34 ① definite   ② potential   ③ upcoming   ④ constant

[Questions 35-38] refer to the following article.

Changes Ahead for Asaro

May 12-As predicted by industry insiders, Asaro has confirmed the __35__ of Michelle Lemke to regional manager for the southwest division.

__36__ Beginning on June 1, she will be taking over her new responsibilities. Along with __37__ contracts with supplier, Lemke will monitor the performance of individual stores and set sales targets.

Lemke started that she plans to introduce changes to boost earning over the next few quarter. __38__ , she wants to add a wider variety of health-related products to the inventory.

The outgoing regional manager, Curtis Lynch, will have company to pursue other professional activities.

---

35 ① earning   ② promotion   ③ replacement   ④ presence

36 ① The decision will be made by Asaro board members at next week's meeting.

② Lemke is currently working as the manager of the pharmacy chain's branch in Phoenix.

③ The Southwest division has generated the least income of all regions in the past quarter.

④ Asaro is gaining market share in key areas as its competitors struggle.

37 ① negotiation   ② negotiate   ③ negotiating   ④ negotiates

38 ① In contrast   ② Otherwise   ③ In particular   ④ Regardless

[Questions 39-42] refer to the following letter.

Ricky Morrow
1265 Elkview Drive
West Palm Beach, FL 33401

Dear MR. Morrow.

I am pleased to inform you that you have been ___39___ to participate in a consumer panel at Bolman's Department Store.

As a frequent shopper at Bolman's and a member of our store rewards club, you can share valuable feedback about products and services. By hearing honest opinions from you and others, we can make sure that the   shopping experience is ___40___ for everyone.

We hope you will also be interested in participating in the panel. ___41___ As compensation for contributing to our research, you will be given a $100   store voucher. ___42___ is no expiration date on the voucher, and it can be   redeemed at any Bolman's location. .

Thank you for your consideration, and we hope to see you soon at Bolman's.

Sincerely,
Devin Everette
Marketing Director, Bolman's Department Store.

---

39 ① settled   ② chosen   ③ sustained   ④ overlooked

40 ① enjoys   ② enjoyable   ③ enjoyment   ④ enjoying

41 ① If so, please call 1-800-BOLMANS to reserve a spot in one of our sessions.

② Otherwise, one of our customer service agents will contact you with details.

③ Given our wide selection, there in something for everyone at our store.

④ Initially, the panel was made up of both employees and shoppers.

42 ① Nothing ② There ③ Each ④ That

[Questions 43-46] refer to the following article.

Historic Theater Celebrates Milestone

SOUTHFIELD-The Southfield Theater is holding a music festival to make its 75th anniversary this summer. Several high-profile singers and dance troupes have already been booked, and the number of __43__ is expected to be about thirty musical groups in total.

The theater's owner, Mona Felton, plans to launch a Web site solely dedicated to the event. __44__ from May 15, the finalized schedule can be viewed on the Web site, and tickets can be purchased online or at the theater's box office.

"We are thankful to be part of a community that is such a strong supporter of the arts," said Felton. To show appreciation to its patrons, the theater __45__ seventy-five tickets to the opening concert. __46__ The deadline for this is May 31.

---

43 ① representatives ② critics ③ listeners ④ performers

44 ① Releasing ② Starting ③ Ordering ④ Transferring

45 ① giving away ② had given away
③ will give away ④ gave away

46 ① Tickets will be sold on a first-come, first-served basis.

② The seats will be in the center of the theater's main floor.

③ People can enter the ticket drawing by submitting a form in the Web site.

④ Patrons will also be served an array of free refreshments during intermission.

[Questions 47-48] refer to the following text message chain.

Tara Jones	19:02

I just got a call from Jessica. She was in an accident while riding her bicycle and broke ankle.

Paul Solse	19:04

I'm so sorry hear that! Is she okay?

Tara Jones	19:06

She needs some time off, but she is scheduled to open the store tomorrow.

Tara Jones	19:07

I need another assistant manager to cover her shift. Can you work from 9 A.M. to 4 P.M for her?

Paul Solse	19:11

Of course. I'm free tomorrow.

Paul Solse	19:20

What other shifts is she supposed to work this week?

Tara Jones	19:22

Wednesday evening and both Saturday and Sunday morning.

Paul Solse	19:24

I can cover all three of those days as well.

47 What can be inferred about Jessica?

① She works fill-time hours.

② She commute to work by bicycle.

③ She has a supervisory role.

④ She is employed in a clothing store.

48 At 19:11, what does Mr. Soles mean when hr writes, "Of course"?

① He sill visit a friend in the hospital.

② He will go to work tomorrow morning.

③ He will find a suitable replacement.

④ He will update a store's employee schedule.

[Questions 49-50] refer to the following form.

Santana Co. Maintenance Request

Requested by	DEPARTMENT NAME Accounting	DEPARTMENT BILLING CODE 116-49	
	NAME Virginia Clark	DATE OF REQUEST Monday, November 15	
	OFFICE LOCATION Room #309	PHONE NUMBER 555-3004	
Work Description	LOCATION OF MAINTENANCE WORK Third floor women's bathroom next to the reception desk	WHEN THE PROBLEM WAS FIRST NOTICED Morning of November 15	
	DESCRIPTION OF NEEDED WORK The sink on the right-hand side has water leaking from its hot water faucet.		
Maintenance Dept. Use Only	WORK ORDER #30684		
	DATE RECEIVED November 15	RECEIVED BY Rafael Jordan	
	NOTES The bathroom has been temporarily closed and the water has been shut off. A professional plumber is scheduled to arrive on Tuesday at 9 A.M. to fix the problem.		
	If you have a question regarding the work status, call 555-3011.		

49 In which department does Rafael Jordan most likely work?

① Accounting　② Maintenance　③ Reception　④ Shipping

50 What is indicated about the problem?

① It requires the help of a professional.

② It was discovered on Monday afternoon.

③ It occurred on the second floor.

④ It will be resolved on November 17.

[Questions 51-52] refer to the following advertisement.

Private Lessons at Sunbeam Martial Arts Studio

Are you looking for a great way to stay in shape? Beginning May 1, Sunbeam Martial Arts Studio will offer one- to five-person private lessons at a flat rate of $120 for 90 minutes. For example, the cost would be $60 each for a two-person group, $40 each for a three-person group, etc. The classes can be scheduled for mornings and afternoons before 5 P.M. We have classes in four types of martial arts:

Wednesdays: Kung Fu
Thursdays: Tai Chi
Fridays: Taekwondo
Saturdays: Karate

You must book your private lesson at least two days in advance. To reserve your spot, or to learn more, please e-mail info@subeamma.com.

---

51 What is indicated about the lessons?

① They are not held in the evening.

② They have a maximum of four people.

③ They last for approximately one hour.

④ They are open to members only.

52 By when must interested parties register for taekwondo lessons?

① By Tuesday　　② By Wednesday　　③ By Thursday　　④ By Friday

[Questions 53-54] refer to the following notice.

NOTICE OF ROAD CLOSURE

This is to notify Arborville motorists that the northbound lanes of Highway 8 will be closed from Layman Street to Berkley Street to undergo annual maintenance work. From June 14 to June 18, traffic will be diverted to Gateway Avenue. No parking will be allowed on Gateway Avenue during this time in order to keep traffic flowing. Please be reminded that the work is expected to cause traffic congestion throughout the area, so motorists should account for delays when calculating their driving times. Updates regarding the project will be announced regularly on radio traffic reports.

---

53 What can be inferred about Gateway Avenue?

① It is a one-way street.

② It passes through a residential zone.

③ It will be closed for maintenance work.

④ It will have heavier traffic than usual.

54 What are motorists reminded to do?

① Reduce their driving speed

② Allow extra time for travel

③ Check for updates online

④ Follow traffic signs carefully

[Questions 55-57] refer to the following memo.

To. All Staff

From: Dennis McCallum, Branch Supervisor

Date: June 2

I would like to announce that Coco Beverages has decided to become a corporate sponsor for an upcoming charity dinner at the Flora Convention Center on June 15 at 7 P.M. Proceeds will be donated to the recently opened Northgate Hospital to support the study of various cancer treatments. We encourage all employees to be in attendance, as the organizers hope to break last year's record of $10,000.

Tickets are $40 per person, and they include wine and a buffet meal. The company will reimburse you for half the price of your ticket, so please keep the receipt. During the dinner, artists will be giving live demonstrations. Their paintings will then be auctioned off at the end of the evening.

You can truly make a positive impact on the lives of others by taking part in this event. If you have any questions, feel free to contact me at extension 29. Thank you.

---

55 Why is the event being held?

① To promote the company's latest beverage

② To raise money for medical research

③ To announce a corporate merger

④ To celebrate a hospital's grand opening

56 The word "break" in paragraph 1, line 6, is closest in meaning to.

① destroy　② rest　③ stop　④ surpass

57 According to the memo, who will be featured at the event?

① Dancers   ② Musicians   ③ Painters   ④ Photographers

[Questions 58-61] refer to the following product manual.

Caring for Your Spinmaster Front-Load Washing Machine

Although front-loading washing machines are quieter, faster, and use less water, they do require special care when cleaning. The watertight rubber seal around the door can occasionally trap moisture, which allows mold to grow. -[1]- This bacteria can then cause the machine to smell slightly. -[2]- The steps listed below will address this issues:

1. **Empty washer:** Take out all clothing from the machine.

2. **Clean rubber seal:** Soak an old towel in hot soapy water and clean the door's rubber seal.

3. **Clean dispensers:** Scrub detergent and fabric softener dispensers to remove product buildup.

4. **Run cleaning cycle:** Pour vinegar into the machine and run an empty wash cycle.

Following these steps regularly should keep your washer clean and door-free. -[3]- An ongoing smell indicates that mold may be growing behind the drum. if not, it's possible that the filter is clogged. -[4]- A qualified repairperson will then come to take apart and clean the machine.

---

58 What is mentioned as a benefit about front-loading washers?

① They cost less to buy than top-loaders.

② They use less laundry detergent.

③ They complete wash cycles more quickly.

④ They are easier to clean.

59 What is NOT listed as a possible cause of door?

① A collection of mildew around the door

② A buildup of detergent in dispenser trays

③ A blocked washing machine filter

④ A growth of mold behind the drum

60 What should users do first if they notice that the machine smells?

① Contact a Spinmaster repairperson

② Remove their clothing from the washer

③ Pour vinegar in the drum of the machine

④ Remove the fabric softener dispenser

61 In which of the positions marked [1], [2], [3], and [4] does the following sentence best belong?

"If odor problems persist after cleaning, please call a Spinmaster expert at 555-903-4862."

① [1]   ② [2]   ③ [3]   ④ [4]

[Questions 62-64] refer to the following job posting.

PART-TIME DRIVE WANTED

Join the team at Thiel, Inc., one of the nation's largest networks of couriers. We have a reputation for reliability and efficiency. Moreover, our employees enjoy generous benefits and excellent working conditions.

Position Summary

The selected applicant will be responsible for dropping off and picking up packages at both residential and commercial sites. The shift begins at 6:30 A.M. on weekdays and ends at approximately 11:30 A.M., depending on the work volume for that day.

Required Qualifications

– Minimum age of 18

– In possession of a valid driver's license

– Strength to lift 30 kilograms without help

– Pasiing score on general health evaluation

– Superb knowledge of the layout of Dayton City and ability to find addresses without relying on a navigation device

To apply for the job, visit our headquarters at 1679 Ashwood Drive to speak with an HR representative. To browse other job openings, visit www.thielinc.com.

62 What type of business is Thiel, Inc.?

① A delivery service ② A tour operator

③ An airport shuttle service ④ A taxi company

63 What is NOT listed as a requirement of the position?

① Being familiar with the metropolitan area

② Having the ability to lift a certain weight

③ Holding a valid driver's license

④ Being free to work on weekends

64 How can people apply for the job?

① By e-mailing an application ② By attending a job fair

③ By filling out an online form ④ By visiting the company's head office

[Questions 65-67] refer to the following e-mail.

To: Asha Kapoor <kapoora@fenelltech.com>
From: Harold seiler <h_seiler@bondsolutions.com>
Date: December 14
Subject: Hello

Dear Asha,

I'm writing to let you know about a position for a full-time Web site designer at my company that you might be interested in. The job won't be publicly advertised until December 20, so you can have the advantage of getting in your resume early. Since I observed your skills and work ethic firsthand while working at Fenell Tech, I would be happy to write you a letter of recommendation.

Attached is a summary of the primary duties of the position. Should you meet the necessary qualifications, which I'm sure you do, you'll be invited for an interview with the team leader. You'll be given information about the salary and benefits at that time.

If you want to apply, please send an e-mail to the human resources director, Leona Addisom, at l_addison@bondsolutions.com. I wish you the best of luck in this process. Please do not hesitate to e-mail me with any questions you may have.

Sincerely,

Harold

65 Why did Mr. Seiler write the e-mail?

① To invite Ms. Kappor to an interview

② To tell about a company's job opening

③ To congratulate Ms. Kappor on a promotion

④ To acknowledge receipt of an application

66 What can be inferred about Mr. Seiler?

① He moved to a different company last month.

② He found an error on a resume.

③ He works as a human resources director.

④ He used to be Ms. Kapoor's coworker.

67 What does Mr. Seiler include with the e-mail?

① A directory of employees

② A letter of recommendation

③ An outline of job responsibilities

④ An interview schedule

[Questions 68-71] refer to the following information.

Meeting Rooms Open to Neighborhood Groups

Rosedale Community Center wishes to announce that the meeting room located to the right of the front entrance is now open to the public to use for free. The meeting room may be reserved for a maximum of three hours at a time by any public group or individual. - [1] -

Room reservation can be made in person at least a day in advance at the center's information desk. It is open between the hours of 10 A.M. abd 6 P.M. - [2] - At the time of booking, a form must be completed with contact information for the group's leader, a summary of the group's purpose, the meeting's expected duration time, and whether or not it will be a recurring event. - [3] -

When using the room, please adhere to the following rules. First, no more than two

---

dozen people can use the meeting room at the same time. Second, beverages with lids are allowed in the room, but food is not permitted. Third, users are asked to clean the room and hit the light switch when they leave. – [4] – Individuals who break these rules may have their use of the space restricted in the future.

Thank you,

Rosedale Community Center

www.rosedalecommunitycenter.com

68 What is mentioned about the meeting room at Rosedale Community Center?

① It should be booked for a full day.

② It was created for business use.

③ It can be reserved at the last-minute.

④ It is available without charge.

69 What are all users required to do before they leave the meeting room?

① Clean up their food waste

② Make sure the lights are off

③ Lock the conference room door

④ Erase any writing on the whiteboard

70 What is NOT necessary information for the reservation form?

① The name of participants

② Meeting start and end times

③ The organizer's phone number

④ A written description of the group

71 In which of the positions marked [1], [2], [3], and [4] does the following sentence best belong?

"Cancellations must be made at least two hours before the start time of the reservation."

① [1]　　② [2]　　③ [3]　　④ [4]

[Questions 72-75] refer to the following notice.

ATTENTION LIBRARY PATRONS

Dominic Lima, the best-selling fiction writer, is returning to our library! In addition to being a successful author himself, Mr. Lima is also a professional writing coach. He has spent the last decade helping inexperienced writers perfect their craft through seminars and workshops. His workshop here last year was such a huge hit that we are very excited to welcome him back a second time.

Mr. Lima's writing workshop will be held from 6 P.M. to 9 P.M. on January 24. During the first hour, he will provide a number of general writing tips and strategies to aspiring novelists. -[1]- Following a short break, the second portion of the workshop will give participants the opportunity to share some of their own work. -[2]- Afterward, Mr. Lima will then give personalized feedback to each of the attendees. -[3]-

Tickets are required for this event. They will be on sale for $15 at the library's circulation desk over the next two weeks. Last-minute attendees will be able to purchase tickets on the day of the workshop, but the cost will go up to $20. Therefore, make sure to buy a ticket early! We highly encourage you to participate in this valuable workshop. -[4]-

---

72 Who is Dominic Lima?

① A reference librarian

② A famous novelist

③ A published poet

④ A literature professor

73 What is scheduled to happen at the event?

① Fiction books will be on sale.

② Participants will review each other's work.

③ Writing advice will be shared by an expert.

④ Refreshments will be provided.

74 Why are people advised to buy tickets early?

① Prices will increase closer to the event.

② The spots for participants are limited.

③ Low interest will cancel the workshop.

④ Front-row tickets will sell out first.

75 In which of the positions marked [1],[2],[3], and [4] does the following sentence best belong?

"Many former participants have gone on to publish books of their own."

① [1]   ② [2]   ③ [3]   ④ [4]

[Questions 76-80] refer to the following schedule and e-mail.

Real to Reel Cinema
HOLIDAY MOVIE WEEK!

It's that time of year again! Christmas is upon us and Real to Reel Cinema wants to help you celebrate. For the week leading up to Christmas, we will be showing some of your favorite Christmas movies each night. Come and re-experience your childhood by watching these classic films! The cost of viewing is free, but we ask all attendees to bring a food item for us to donate to our local food bank. All items can be placed under the Christmas tree in the lobby.

Check the schedule below to see what we have planned for you!

MONDAY	TUESDAY	WEDNESDAY	THURSDAY	FRIDAY
December 21	December 22	December 23	Christmas Eve	Christmas Day
Christmas Bells	A Special Christmas Eve	This Christmas	A Becker Town Christmas	Winter Wishes
An iconic romantic musical.	A black-and-white comedy.	A holiday classic about a special boy.	The holiday episode from a TV show.	Four dramatic version of a famous novel.

· Two viewings will be held nightly for each film at 7:30 P.M. and 10:00 P.M.

· The film on Thursday can be attended by children of all ages who are accompanied by an adult. To accommodate this younger audience, the film will hold a third viewing at 4:30 P.M.

· No Christmas is complete without Winter Wishes. Therefore, we have planned a full day for this film alone. There will be four versions shown every 2.5 hours on Christmas Day. The first viewing will begin at 11:00 A.M.

To: <info@r2rcinema.com>

From: Euan Cassidy <cassidy@usermail.net>

Date: December 27

Subject: Christmas Day movie marathon

To whom it may concern,

I am sending this e-mail as a follow up to your Christmas movie promotion. I attended the early showing of Winter Wishes on December 25. I very much like the idea of having a movie marathon of Christmas Day, but I have a small suggestion on how it could be improved. Instead of showing many different versions of the same movie all in one day, I think it might be a little bit more interesting to watch several different movies. I hope that you will take this into consideration when planning next year's event.

Best regards,

Euan Cassidy

76 What type of film is A Special Christmas Eve?

① A drama ② A romance ③ A comedy ④ A musical

77 What are viewers asked to leave at the theater?

① Food items for donation   ② Wrapped Christmas presents
③ Proof of purchase for tickets ④ Ornaments for a Christmas tree

78 What is different about the movie on Thursday?

① It will be shown in black and white.

② It is based on a famous piece of literature.

③ It is intended specifically for children.

④ It will be played in multiple versions.

79 Why did Mr. Cassidy write the e-mail?

① To recommend a change to movie times

② To make a suggestion about film choices

③ To thank the cinema for holding an event

④ To inquire about an item left in a theater

80 At what time did Mr. Cassidy see a movie?

① 4:30 P.M.   ② 6:30 P.M   ③ 10:00 P.M.   ④ 11:00 A.M.

[Questions 81-85] refer to the following letter and e-mail.

FINE FABRIC MARKET — Jingumae, Shibuya-ku, Tokyo, Japan

15 November

Mr. Manuel Sanz

Vestigia Decor

Holanda 3745

RM Nunoa, Chile

Dear Mr. Sanz:

As a leading wholesaler of rare and high-quality fabrics, we have proudly sold to interior design companies around the world for over a decade. We would like to inform you that we have recently transitioned from issuing print product catalogs to a digital catalog. Oue digital catalog will be available at the beginning of December.

Until then, here are a few highlights of our exclusive new products (swatches are enclosed):

"Climb" (Item 462): This traditional design suggests a series of interlocking ladders. The finest polished cotton; blue and yellow.

"Morning" (Item 517): Based on an ancient motif, this design depicts clouds rising from a mountain at sunrise. Silk damas; white and brown.

"Circles" (Item 614): The round flower pattern was inspired by shapes on a nineteenth-century gown. Linen; violet, beige, and green.

"Phase" (Item 628): This exquisue pattern suggests the phase of the moon and is belived to have origins on Western Asia. Wool; gold and midnight blue.

As a bonus to our valued customers, we are currently offering a 15 percent discount on orders of any particular fabric over 20 meters. We look forward to your continued business.

Sincerely,

Kentaro Manabe

Kentaro Manabe, Sales Director

To: kmanabe@FFMt.com
From: msanz@vestigia.cl
Date: 20 November

Subject: Today's order

Dear Mr. Manabe:

Following our cinversation of earlier today, I wish to conform my order of 12 meters of "Climb," Item 462, and 26 meters of "Morning," Item 517. As I mentioned, we are considering a third fabric, "Phase," which would look very nice on a popular model of our occasional chairs. However, my business partner has some concerns with the fabric's weave, as we have had issues in the past with tearing and fraying in upholstering these chairs. The sample swatch that you sent is rather smaill. If possible, please forward a larger sample of this product to us so that we may make a determination of the fabric's suitability.

Regards,

Manuel Sanz

---

81 What does the letter indicated about Fine Fabric Market?

① It is under new management.

② It publishes a new catalog annually.

③ Its headquarters is relocating to Chile.

④ It sells products directly to other businesses.

82 What is true about all the fabrics listed in the letter?

① Their designs have many colors.

② Their cost will increase in December.

③ They were manufactured in South America.

④ They were designed by one artist.

83 For which fabric will Mr. Sanz receive a discount?

① Climb   ② Morning   ③ Circles   ④ Phases

84 What is Ms. Sanz's business partner worried about?

① The delay of a previous order ② The express shipping costs

③ The qualities of a particular fabric ④ The availability of an item

85 What does Mr. Sanz want Mr. Manabe to do?

① Repair the damaged chairs

② Change the product that was ordered

③ Send him another fabric sample

④ Consider becoming his business consultant

[Question 86-90] refer to the following advertisement, online shopping cart and e-mail.

Natural Pets makes shopping for your animals easy! We sell cat and dog food in a variety of flavors and sizes. Rather than buying large bags of various types to determine if your animal(s) will like them, we allow you to experiment for free. Simply scroll through the options on our Web site and choose sample flavors to try. Whether you are ordering for your own pet or for a clinic, you can order online, and it will be delivered to you the next day.

*Some customers will be eligible for a "loyalty" discount of 15%. The discount will be added automatically to the orders of customers who shop with us at least once a month.

www.naturalpets.com/shoppingcart			
Customer Name: Aaron Fincham			
Order Number: 4354			
Item	Weight	Quantity	Price
Natural Dog - turkey DF-535	4 lb	4	$128.00
Natural Dog - salmon DF-576	sample	1	$0.00
Natural Dog - beef DF-642	sample	1	$0.00
Natural Dog - chicken PF-787	4 lb	2	$64.00
Subtotal			$192.00
Applied discount (15%)			$28.80
Total			$163.20

To: Customer Service <cs@naturalpets.com>

From: Aaron Fincham <aaron_fincham@fleetwoodrescue.com>

Date: April 22

Subject: Order #4354

To whom it may concern,

I received order #4354 yesterday. I placed the standard order for my dog rescue facility, and I even took advantage of your promotion to try a few new food flavors. I paid for DF-535, but DF-353 (lamb) was inside the box. The product numbers are so similar that I understand how the mistake may have happened. Could you please send the correct bag of food for me? Also, could you send a full bag of DF-642? The sample flavor was the top choice among the dogs here, and I want to order more of it.

Thank you,

Aaron Fincham

Office Administrator, Fleetwood Dog Rescue

86 What does Natural Pets encourage its customers to do?

① Buy in bulk to save money

② Visit the store to pick up orders

③ Test out samples before purchase

④ Visit a clinic at least once a month

87 What can be inferred about Mr. Fincham?

① He chose to pay for express shipping.

② He purchased food for his personal animals.

③ He shops frequently with Natural Pets.

④ He placed two separate orders.

88 What type of food does Mr. Fincham request more of?

① Turkey   ② Salmon   ③ Beef   ④ Chicken

89 What mistakes was made with order 4354?

① One of the requested items didn't arrive.

② The total on the invoice was incorrect.

③ It was delivered to the wrong address.

④ The parcel was damaged during shipment.

90 In the e-mail, the word "top" in paragraph 1, line 5 is closest in meaning to

① important   ② upper   ③ maximum   ④ favorite

[Question 91-95] refer to the following schedule, review, and article.

The Bilbridge Arts Institute (BAI)Fall Course Schedule

Photography Basics (6:00 PM to 8:00 PM)Mondays in September	Ceramics I (6:00 PM to 8:00 PM) Fridays in October
Ceramics II (5:00 PM to 8:00 PM) Tuesdays in November	Painting (6:30 PM to 8:30 PM) Thursdays in December

Visit www.bai.edu/classes for a detailed description of topics covered. For those classes that require students to purchase supplies, a supply list is included with the description.

Registration accepted online and on person. Course fee: $125 for residents of Algonville; $140 for nonresidents.

---

http://www.bai.edu/reviews

I was initially hesitant to sign up to spend my Friday nights in a pottery studio instead of with family and friends. However, after just 30 minutes in Mr.Qabbani's class, I knew that I'd made the right decision. His sense of humor and interactive teaching style made thee experience a lot of fun! Both my confidence and interest in pottery grew with every piece I made. In fact, my creations turned out so well that they will be featured during the BAI's upcoming open house. I couldn't have been surprised . . . and proud!

-Melissa Brumfield

91 What do all of the BAI's classes have in common?

① They begin at the same time.

② They are three hours long.

③ They cost less for Algonville residents.

④ They require students to buy materials.

92 Who most likely is Mr.Qabbani?

① A BAI instructor

② A friend of Ms.Brumfield

③ The owner of a pottery studio

④ The organizer of the BAI's open house

93 When did Ms.Brumfield take a course at the BAI?

① In September   ② In October   ③ In November   ④ In December

94 What is indicated about Ms.Brumfield?

① She published an article in November.

② She will have her work displayed in December.

③ She plans to take another BAI course.

④ She learned about the BAI at an open house event.

95 What does the article suggest about the BAI?

① It employs a local public relations company.

② It recently increased its advertising efforts.

③ It holds open house events throughout the year.

④ It has been offering arts programs for fifteen years.

[Questions 96-100] refer to the following e-mails and Web page.

E-Mail Message
To: Marcello Rosillo
From: Svetlana Ridic
Date: February 19
Subject: Design notes

Dear Marcello,

I'd like your design group to deal with a few issues as we make modifications to the CR 465. First, note that updated government emissions regulations for motorcycles come out this week, so the design will need to address any changes that are new. Also, riders of the current model have reported that rear visibility is a weakness of the design. The size of the mirrors should be adjusted to address this problem. Finally, bikes that are more than two years old seem to have trouble with fading paint.

The design phase must be completed by June 8. The deadline is firm this time around—manufacturing does not want to face the same time and budget issues it had to deal with last year.

The market is healthy for this type of bike, and this is a great opportunity for Roadwell Motorcycles to strengthen our reputation. As with previous CR 465 models, we will continue to focus on creating quality products rather than on beating our competitors' prices.

Thanks,

Svetlana

E-Mail Message
To: Svetlana Ridic
From: Marcello Rosillo
Date: February 20
Subject: Design notes
Dear Svetlana,
We received advance notice of the regulations yesterday. We were already planning to give the bike a longer wheelbase, which will add another 5kg to its weight. Modifying the exhaust system to meet the new regulations will increase the weight by an additional 5kg. The total increase of 10kg is enough to be a significant worry if we want to ensure smooth handling. However, I am confident that we can solve this problem well in advance of the deadline.
We are also looking at using a new product with UV protection to keep it looking shiny. I'll get back to you with my views on manufacturing costs; I don't expect the design changes to have a radical impact.
Best,
Marcello

http://www.goroadreviews.com
Mini-review:
Roadwell CR 465
★★★★
The newest model of this attractive bike debuted from Roadwell Motorcycles in October. I took it for a ride in dry conditions and performed beautifully, handling corners smoothly and stopping without slipping. The larger mirrors on this year's model gave me a much better view of vehicles coming up behind me. This bike has a slightly different feel from last year's machine, probably because it weighs in at 10 kilograms heavier. Roadwell has designed several new options for the

bike's trim and its handlebar, and the bike is available in a greater variety of colors. Pricing is comparable to last year's model.

By Tom333

96 What does Ms. Ridic suggest about Mr. Rossillo's department?

① It recently revised its budget.　② It missed a deadline previously.
③ It updates designs every two years.　④ It surveyed riders about the CR 465.

97 What does Mr. Rossilo express concern about?

① Additional manufacturing costs　② The motorcycle's overall weight
③ The lack of available paint colors　④ Changes to the production schedule

98 Which issue related to the redesign does Mr. Rossilo fail to address in his e-mail?

① Mirror size　② Upgraded paint
③ Emissions regulations　④ Wheelbase dimensions

99 What does the reviewer indicate about his experience with the CR 465?

① He thought the bike was too heavy.
② He was not happy with the paint choices.
③ He could not test-drive this year's model.
④ He found that its rear visibility had been improved.

100 What is most likely true about the newest model of the CR 465?

① It performs best in wet conditions.
② Its paint will begin to fade after two years.
③ It costs more than competitors' products.
④ It offers fewer trim options than older models.

◆ 정답 및 해설

▶ **[정답]**

1	2	3	4	5	6	7	8	9	10
②	①	④	②	④	④	①	②	③	④
11	12	13	14	15	16	17	18	19	20
②	③	③	④	③	①	①	④	③	②
21	22	23	24	25	26	27	28	29	30
①	②	①	③	①	②	③	②	①	④
31	32	33	34	35	36	37	38	39	40
④	①	③	③	②	②	③	③	②	②
41	42	43	44	45	46	47	48	49	50
①	②	④	②	③	③	③	②	②	①
51	52	53	54	55	56	57	58	59	60
①	②	③	②	②	④	③	③	②	②
61	62	63	64	65	66	67	68	69	70
④	①	④	④	②	④	③	④	②	①
71	72	73	74	75	76	77	78	79	80
③	②	③	①	④	③	①	③	②	④
81	82	83	84	85	86	87	88	89	90
④	①	②	③	③	③	③	③	①	④
91	92	93	94	95	96	97	98	99	100
③	①	②	②	④	②	②	①	④	③

▶ **해설**

1. (해석) 산토스 씨는 막판에 계획이 바뀌는 바람에 교통편을 직접 예매해야
   했다.
   [어휘] book: 예매하다 transportation: 교통(편) last-minute: 마지막 순간의,
   막바지의

2. (해석) 회계직 지원서는 늦어도 4월 19일까지는 접수되어야 합니다.
   [어휘] application: 지원(서) accounting: 회계 position: 직위, 자리 receive:
   받다, 접수하다 no later than: 늦어도

3. (해석) 더 많은 관광객을 유치하기 위해 헨리 박물관은 7월에 무료 입장을
제공하고 있다.

[어휘] in order to+동사원형: ~하기 위해서 attract: 유인하다, 끌어들이다
tourist: 관광객 admission: 입장

4. (해석) 1월 1일에 기차 승차권 금액이 소폭 인상될 예정이다.

[어휘] be set to+동사원형: ~할 예정이다 increase: 상승하다, 증가하다
slightly: 약간, 조금 urgently: 긴급하게 equally: 똑같이, 동등하게

5. (해석) 회사는 장기근속에 대한 감사로 패리다 씨에게 은퇴 기념 파티를 열
어 주었다.

[어휘] appreciate: 감사, 이해 throw a party: 파티를 열다 retirement: 은퇴

6. (해석) 이 지리정보로 애플리케이션은 사용자의 위치를 자동으로 추적해 가
장 빠른 경로를 결정한다.

[어휘] automatically: 자동으로 track: 추적하다 position: 위치 determine:
결정하다, 판단하다.

7. (해석) 반품되는 물품에는 소정의 재입고 수수료가 부과되며 이는 고객님의
환불금에서 공제됩니다.

[어휘] incur: (손해 등을) 초래하다, (비용 등을) 물게 되다. minimal: 최소
의 restock: 다시 채워 넣다 deduct A from B: B에서 A를 공
제하다 refund: 환불(금)

8. (해석) 양측이 서류에 서명하면 계약이 발효된다.

[어휘] agreement: 계약, 합의 effective: 발효[시행]되는, 효과적인 party:
(계약 등의) 당사자 document: 문서, 서류

9. (해석) 앨리스 그리솜 주방장은 자신이 스트라스부르그에 레스토랑을 추가

- Part 4 토익 실전문제(100 문제) 193

로 개업할지, 아니면 그대로 콜마르에만 남을지를 결정해야 한다고 말한다.

[어휘] chef: 요리사 decide: 결정[결심]하다 additional: 추가의 remain: 남다, 계속 ~이다

10. (해석) 쉐필드 시네마는 최고의 해외 영화와 독립 영화를 선보이는 데 주력한다.

[어휘] focus on: ~에 초점을 맞추다. present: 제시하다, 보여주다 independent: 독립적인 refer: 조회하다, 맡기다 occur: 발생하다.

11. (해석) 이사회에 참석한 사람들만 그 사안에 대해 투표할 수 있다.

[어휘] present: 참석한, 출석한 board of directors: 이사회 vote: 투표하다 issue: 쟁점, 사안

12. (해석) 공학부는 단발 엔진 항공기의 부품 사양을 검토하는 과정에 있다.

[어휘] division: 부서 in the process of: ~의 과정에서 specifications: 사양, 설명서 aircraft: 항공기 interest: 관심, 흥미 custom: 관습

13. (해석) 라바날 씨는 법인세를 다룬 경험이 아주 풍부한데, 그중 대부분이 지방세 관련 경력이다.

[어휘] a great deal: 아주 많은 experience: 경험, 경력 corporate: 기업의 taxation: 조세 local: 지방의

14. (해석) 금융 예측가들의 전망에도 불구하고 올머 퓨엘 코퍼레이션의 전체 매출은 10퍼센트 증가했다.

[어휘] prediction: 전망, 예측 financial: 재무의, 금융의 forecaster: 예측가, overall: 전반적인, 전체의

15. (해석) 개정된 고용 계약서는 월말에 배포될 예정입니다.

[어휘] revised: 개정된, 수정된 employment: 고용 contract: 계약(서); 계약

하다 distribute: 배포하다

16. (해석) 기업들은 종종 계약업체와 협력하여 공통의 우려 사항에 대한 해결책을 찾는다.

   [어휘] collaborate with: ~와 협력하다 contractor: 계약업체, 도급업체 solution: 해결책, 해법 shared: 공유하는, 공통된 concern: 걱정 evaluate: 평가하다 conduct: 수행하다 support: 지지[지원]하다

17. (해석) 알루키안 씨는 지속적으로 고품질의 작품을 만들어 낸다.

   [어휘] consistently: 지속적으로, 일관되게 produce: 만들다, 제작하다 high-quality: 양질의, 고품질의

18. (해석) 차이 씨의 지난달 관광 매출은 예상했던 것을 훨씬 넘어섰다.

   [어휘] anticipate: 예상하다, 기대하다 considering: ~을 고려[감안]하면

19. (해석) 눈썰미 있는 방문자라면 시맨티카 인더스트리즈에서 많은 직원이 서서 컴퓨터로 일하고 있는 모습에 주목할 것이다.

   [어휘] observant: 관찰력 있는 notice: 인지하다, 주목하다 employee: 직원 observable: 눈에 잘 띄는

20. (해석) 나주 인터내셔널이 아산 솔루션즈를 인수하자 어제 나주사 주가가 급등했다.

   [어휘] acquisition: 인수 cause: 야기하다; 원인 stock price: 주가 soar: 급등하다, 치솟다 drawback: 결점 provision: 공급, 제공 indicator: 지수, 지표

21. (해석) 구매 영수증은 이제 전자식으로 발행되어 고객에게 이메일로 전송됩니다.

   [어휘] purchase: 구매(품); 구매하다 receipt: 영수증 generate: 만들어 내다, 창출하다 electronically: 전자식으로 customer: 고객, 소비자

22. (해석) 해산물 가공 처리 리례가 생선을 손질하고 나면 그것을 판매용으로 포장한다.

    [어휘] processor: 가공처리기계   package: 포장하다

23. (해석) 모니터의 밝기는 화면의 이미지를 보기에 적합하도록 조정할 수 있습니다.

    [어휘] adjust: 조정하다   brightness: 밝기 suitable for: ~에 적합한 view: 보다

24. (해석) 야마토 박사가 이미 떠난다고 밝혔으므로 이사회는 곧 후임자를 시급히 지면해야 한다.

    [어휘] announce: 발표하다 departure: 출발 imperative: 시급한 board: 이사회   name: 지명하다 successor: 후임자 sincere: 진심 어린 equivalent: 동등한 theoretical: 이론적인

25. (해석) 사무실 직원 수가 곧 두 배로 늘어나게 되므로, 추가로 인쇄기를 설치해야 할지도 모릅니다.

    [어휘] double: 두 배가 되다 install: 설치하다 additional: 추가의

26. (해석) 사진들은 여러 해에 걸친 사회의 발전상을 반영하기 위해 연대순으로 전시된다.

    [어휘] display: 전시하다 chronologically: 연대순으로 reflect: 반영하다 progression: 진행, 발전 extremely: 극도로 biologically: 생물학적으로 actually: 실제로

27. (해석) 멜닉자크 씨가 오늘 오후에 있었던 고객 회의의 회의록은 퇴근 전에 배포할 예정입니다.

    [어휘] distribute: 배포하다 minutes: 회의록, 의사록 client: 고객

28. (해석) 세계가 그것의 아름다운 해변에 대해 더 많이 알게 되면서 사우스 조리에서 관광업이 발달했다.

[어휘] tourism: 관광업   flourish: 번창하다, 번성하다.

29. (해석) 티브의 최고경영자 정 박 씨는 회사가 가까운 미래에 지속 가능한 방식으로 냉장고를 계속 생산하게 되기를 바란다고 말했다.

[어휘] continue: 계속하다 refrigerator: 냉장고 sustainably: 지속 가능한 방식으로 foreseeable: 예견할 수 있는

30. (해석) 메리트 씨늬 시애틀 방문 일정이 매년 열리는 중소 기업 엑스포와 겹쳐서 다행입니다.

[어휘] fortunate: 운이 좋은, 다행인 coincide with: ~와 일치하다, 동시에 일어나다 annual: 해마다 일어나는 access: 접근하다 confirm: 확인하다 accept: 받아들이다

[31-34] (해석)
수신: 전 직원
발신: 레오 길렌

직원들의 의견에 부응하여, 경영 관리팀에서는 휴가사용 절차를 변경하기로 결정했습니다.

이전에는 휴가를 내려면 최소 2주 던 통지가 요구되었고, 이러한 엄격한 규정의 결과로 여러 번 휴가 요청이 거절되었습니다. 새로운 규정 하에서는 자리를 비우는 것을 미리 관리자에게 승인만 받으면, 직원들은 아무 때나 자유롭게 휴가를 사용할 수 있습니다.

그러므로, 급하게 자리를 비워야 할 경우, 이제 허용될 수 있습니다. 팀과 필요한 합의를 하는 것만 확실히 해 주십시오. 더 자세한 내용은 다가오는 회의에서 소개될 것입니다. 이 변경이 여러분 모두에게 유익하기를 바랍니다.

[어휘] respond to: ~에 부응하다 procedure: 절차 vacation leave: 휴가 previously: 이전에 notice: 통지, 공지 require: 요구하다 take time off: 휴가를 내다 request: 요청 reject: 거절하다 on many occasions: 여러 차례 strict: 엄격한 policy: 규정, 방침 feel free to do: 자유롭게 ~하다 as long as: ~하기만 하면 absence: 부재 approve: 승인하다 in advance: 미리 make an arrangement with: ~와 합의하다 upcoming: 다가오는 benefit from: ~로부터 이익을 얻다

32. ① 규정, 방침 ② 분석 ③ 요인 ④증상, 징후
33. ① 마찬가지로 일부 부서들은 다른 부서들보다 인력 부족과 관련된 문제가 더 많습니다.
   ② 특히, 휴가 일정은 휴게실에 매주 게시될 것입니다. ③ 그러므로 급하게 자리를 비워야 할 경우, 이제 허용될 수 있습니다. ④ 이제부터 관리부 팀원들이 이 문제를 팀 차원에서 논의할 것 입니다.

34. ① 확실한 ② 가능성 있는 ③ 다가오는 ④ 끊임없는

[35-38] (해석)
아사로 사의 향후 변화

5월 12일- 업계 내부의 관계자들이 예측한 대로, 아사로 사는 남서부 자국의 지역 매니저에 마셸렘케의 승진을 공식화했다.
렘케 씨는 현재 그 체인 약국의 피닉스 지점 매니저로 일하고 있다. 6월 1일부터 그녀는 새로운 업무를 인계 받게 될 것이다. 공급업체와 계약을 협상하는 것과 더불어, 렘케 씨는 각 매장 실적을 모니터하고 판매 목표를 수립할 것이다.
렘케 씨는 향후 몇 분기 동안 수익을 향상시키기 위해 몇 가지 변화를 도입 할 계획이라고 말했다.
특히 그녀는 더 다양한 건강 관련 제품을 제품 목록에 추가하기를 원하고 있다.

지역 매니저 자리에서 떠나는 커티스 린치는 이 회사를 떠나 다른 전문 활동을 찾을 예정이다.

[어휘] ahead: 향후의 predict: 예측하다 insider: 내부자 confirm: 공식화하다, 확정하다 promotion: 승진 regional: 지역의 division: 분할 take over: 인계 받다 responsibility: 업무, 책임 negotiate: 협상하다 supplier: 공급업자 performance: 실적 individual: 각, 개별의 state: 말하다 boost: 향상시키다 earnings: 수익 in particular: 특히 a wide variety of: 매우 다양한 inventory: 물품 목록, 재고 out going: 떠나는 pursue: 추구하다 professional: 전문적인

35. ① 수익 ② 승진 ③ 교체, 대체 ④ 존재, 참석

36. ① 그 결정은 다음 주 회의에서 아사로사 이사진들에 의해 이루어질 것이다.
   ② 렘케씨는 현재 그 체인 약국의 피닉스 지점 매니저로 일하고 있다.
   ③ 남서부 지국은 지난 분기에 전 지역에서 가장 적은 수익을 냈다.
   ④ 아사로사는 경쟁업체들이 고전함에 따라 주요 지역들에서 시장 점유율을 늘리고 있다.

38. ① 대조적으로 ② 그렇지 않으면 ③ 특히 ④ 개의치 않고

[39-42] (해석)
33401 플로리다 주 웨스트팜 비치
엘크뷰 로 1265번지
리키 모로우

모로우 씨께,

고객님께서 볼먼 백화점의 소비자 패널 참여자로 선정되셨음을 알려드리게 되어 기쁩니다.

볼먼 백화점의 단골이자 저희 백화점 보상클럽의 회원으로서, 고객님께서는 제품 및 서비스에 대해 소중한 의견을 나눠주실 수 있습니다. 고객님을 비롯한 여러 분들의 솔직한 의견을 청취함으로써, 저희는 쇼핑 경험이 모든 분들께 반드시 즐거운 일이 될 수 있도록 하겠습니다.

고객님께서도 패널 참여에 관심이 있으시길 바랍니다. 만약 그러시다면, 1-800-BOLMANS로 전화하셔서 저희 행사 시간 중 하나에 자리를 예약하시기 바랍니다. 저희 조사에 기여해주신 데 대한 보상으로, 100달러짜리 상품권을 받으시게 됩니다. 상품권에는 만료일이 없으며, 볼먼 백화점의 어느 지점에서도 사용 가능합니다.

관심에 감사드리며, 볼먼 백화점에서 조만간 뵙기를 바랍니다.

볼먼 백화점, 마케팅 이사
데빈 에버렛 드림

[어휘] inform: A that~ A에게 ~를 알리다: participate in: ~에 참여하다 consumer panel: 소비자 패널 frequent shopper: 단골고객 rewards club: 보상클럽 valuable: 귀중한 make sure that: 반드시 ~하다 spot: 자리 compensation: 보상 contribute to: ~에 기여하다 voucher: 상품권 expiration: 만료 redeem: 상품과 교환하다 location: 장소 consideration: 관심

39. ① 정착하다, 해결하다 ② 선택하다 ③ 지속시키다 ④ 내려다보다

41. ① 만약 그러시다면, 1-800-BOLMANS로 전화하셔서 저희 행사 시간 중 하나에 자리를 예약하시기 바랍니다.

② 그렇지 않으면 저희 고객서비스 담장 직원이 고객님께 전화드려서 자세한 사항을 알려드릴 것입니다.

③ 다양하게 갖춰진 저희 상품들을 고려해 볼 때, 백화점에서 누구나 원하는 걸 찾을 수 있습니다.

④ 원래, 패널은 직원과 쇼핑객 둘 다로 구성되어 있었습니다.

[43-46] (해석)

역사적인 극장에서 중대한 사건을 기념하다

사우스필드-사우스필드 극장은 올 여름 75주년을 기념하기 위해 음악제를 개최한다. 몇몇 인기 가수와 무용단이 이미 예약되었고, 공연자 숫자는 총 서른 개 가량의 음악 단체에 이를 것으로 예상된다.

극장 주인 모나 펠튼은 이 행사만을 전담하는 웹사이트를 개설 할 계획이다. 5월 15일부터 최종 일정을 웹사이트에서 열람할 수 있으며, 표는 인터넷이나 극장 매표소에서 구입할 수 있다.

"우리는 그토록 열렬히 예술을 지지하는 지역사회의 일원이 될 수 있어 감사하다"라고 펠튼 씨는 말했다. 후원자들에게 감사를 표하기 위해, 극장은 개막 공연이 75장의 표를 무료로 나눠줄 예정이다. 사람들은 웹사이트에 있는 양식을 제출함으로써 표 추첨에 참여할 수 있다. 이 행사의 마감일은 5월 31일이다.

[어휘] historic: 역사적인 celebrate: 기념하다, 축하하다 milestone: 중대한 사
건 hold: 열다 mark: 기념하다 축하하다 high-profile: 매우 주목 받는
dance troupe: 무용단 book: 예약하다 solely: 오로지 appreciation:
감사 patron: 후원자 give away: 기부하다

43. ① 대표, 대리인 ② 평론가 ③ 청취자 ④ 공연자

44. ① 공개하다 ② 시작하다 ③ 주문하다 ④ 이동하다

46. ① 표는 선착순으로 판매된다.

② 좌석은 극장 1층 중앙에 마련된다.

③ 사람들은 웹사이트에 있는 양식을 제출함으로써 표 추첨에 참여할 수 있다.

④ 후원자들에게는 또한 중간 휴식 시간 동안 무료로 다양한 다과가 제공된다.

[47-48] (해석)

타라존스	19:02
제시카에게서 방금 전화를 받았어요. 자전거를 타다 사고가 나서 발목이 부러졌대요..	
폴 솔스	19:04
그런 소식을 들으니 정말 유감이에요! 제시카는 괜찮대요?	
타라존스	19:06
휴가를 내야 하는데, 그녀가 내일 매장을 열기로 되어 있거든요.	
타라존스	19:07
다른 부 매니저가 그녀 대신 근무를 해줘야 해서요. 오전 9시부터 오후 4시까지 그녀 대신 일해 줄 수 있어요?	
폴 솔스	19:11
물론이죠. 전 내일 한가해요.	
폴 솔스	19:20
그녀가 이번 주에 일하기로 되어 있는 다른 근무는 뭐예요?	
타라존스	19:22
수요일 저녁하고 토요일과 일요일 이틀 아침이요.	
폴 솔스	19:24
그 3일간도 제가 모두 대신할 수 있어요.	

[어휘] time off 휴가 be scheduled to do ~하기로 되어 있다 assistant manager 부 매니저 cover 대신하다 shift 교대 근무

47. 제시카에 대해 추론할 수 있는 것은?

① 전일제로 일한다.　　② 자전거를 타고 직장에 통근한다.

③ 관리직을 맡고 있다.　　④ 의류 매장에서 일한다.

48. 19시 11분에, 솔스 씨가 "Of course"라고 말한 것에서 그가 의도한 것은?

① 병원에 있는 친구를 방문하겠다.

② 내일 아침에 일하러 가겠다.

③ 적합한 후임을 찾겠다.

④ 매장의 직원 일정표를 업데이트 하겠다.

[49-50]

산타나 사 유지보수 요청서

	부서명	부서 청구서 발송 코드	
	회계		116-49
	성명	요청일	
	버지니아 클락	11월 15일, 월요일	
	사무실 위치　309호	전화번호　555-3004	
	유지보수 작업 장소	문제가 처음 발견된 시기	
	접수대 옆 3층 여자 화장실	11월 15일 아침	
	필요한 작업 설명		
	오른쪽 개수대의 온수 꼭지애서 물이 샙니다.		
	작업 주문 번호　#30684		
	접수일	접수인	
	11월 15일	라파엘 조단	
	비고		
	화장실은 일시적으로 폐쇄되었고, 수도가 차단되었습니다. 전문 배관공이 문제를 해결하기 위해 화요일 아침 9시에 도착할 예정입니다.		
작업 현황에 관해서 질문이 있는 경우, 555-3011로 전화 바랍니다.			

[어휘] maintenance 유지보수 request 요청 department 부서 accounting. 회계 billing 청구서 발부 reception desk 접수대 description 기술 leak 새다 faucet 수도꼭지 temporarily 일시적으로 shut off 차단하다 professional 전문적인 plumber 배관공 fix 수리하다 regarding ~에 관해서

49. 라파엘 조단은 어느 부서에서 일할 것 같은가?
    ① 회계   ② 관리   ③ 접수   ④ 배송

50. 문제점에 대해서 나타나 있는 바는?
    ① 전문가의 도움을 필요로 한다.   ② 월요일 오후에 발견되었다.
    ③ 2층에서 발생했다.   ④ 11월 17일에 해결될 예정이다.

[51-52] (해석)
선빔 무술 스튜디오에서의 개인 강습

체력을 유지할 좋은 방법을 찾고 계십니까? 5월 1일부터 선빔 무술 스튜디오에서 90분간 120달러의 고정 요금으로 한 명에서 다섯 명까지로 이루어진 개인 강습을 마련합니다. 예를 들어 두 명으로 이루어진 그룹은 비용이 60달러가 될 것이고, 세 명으로 이루어진 그룹은 각자 40달러가 되는 식입니다. 강습은 오후 5시 이전에 오전반과 오후반들로 짜여 질 수 있습니다. 우리는 네 종류의 무술 강좌를 마련하고 있습니다.

수요일: 쿵푸
목요일: 태극권
금요일: 태권도
토요일: 가라테

개인 강습은 적어도 이틀 정에 미리 예약해야 합니다. 자라를 예약하거나 더 자세히

알아보시려면, info@sunbeamma.com으로 이메일을 주십시오.

[어휘] private lesson: 개인 강습 martial arts: 무술 look for: ~를 찾다 stay in shape: 건강한 체력을 유지하다 flat rate: 고정 요금 at least: 최소한 in advance: 미리 reserve: 예약하다 spot: 자리

51. 강습에 대해서 나타나 있는 바는?

① 저녁에는 열리지 않는다.   ② 최대 인원은 네 명이다.

③ 약 한 시간 동안 지속된다.   ④ 회원에게만 개방되어 있다.

52. 관심 있는 사람은 언제까지 태권도 강습을 신청해야 하는가?

① 화요일   ② 수요일   ③ 목요일   ④ 금요일

[53-54] (해설)

도로 폐쇄 공지

본 공지는 아버빌의 운전자들에게 8번 고속도로의 북쪽 방면 도로들이 연례 보수 작업을 받기 위해 레이맨 가에서 부터 버클리 가까지 폐쇄될 것임을 알려드리기 위한 것입니다. 6월 14일부터 6월 18일까지, 교통은 게이트웨이 가로 우회될 것입니다. 이 기간 동안 교통의 흐름을 원활히 하기 위해서 게이트웨이 가에서는 주차가 전혀 허용되지 않습니다. 작업으로 이 지역 도처에서 교통 혼잡이 유발될 것이라는 점을 다시 한 번 염두에 두시길 바라며, 운전자들은 운전 시간을 계산할 때 지체를 고려해야 합니다. 작업에 관한 최신 소식은 라디오 교통 보도에서 정기적으로 안내될 것입니다.

[어휘] notice: 공지 closure: 폐쇄 notify: 알리다 motorist: 운전자 northbound: 북쪽으로 향하는 lane: 도로 close: 폐쇄하다 undergo: 겪다 annual: 연례의 divert: 우회시키다 flow: 흐르다 Please be reminded that :~임을 염두에 두세요   cause: 유

발하다 traffic congestion: 교통 혼잡 throughout: ~도처에 account for: ~을 고려

하다 calculate: 계산하다 regarding: ~에 관한 regularly: 정기적으로

53. 게이트웨이 가에 대한 추론인 것은?

① 일방통행 도로이다.   ② 주거 지역을 통과한다.

③ 보수 작업을 위해 폐쇄될 것이다.   ④ 평소보다 교통량이 많아질 것이다.

54. 운전자들에게 당부하는 것은?

① 운전 속도를 줄일 것   ② 이동에 여유 시간을 가질 것

③ 인터넷에서 최신 소식을 확인할 것   ④ 교통신호를 주의 깊게 따를 것

[55-57] (해석)

수신: 전 직원

발신: 지점 감독관, 데니스 맥컬럼

날짜: 6월 2일

코코 음료는 6월 15일 저녁 7시에 플로라 컨벤션 센터에서 열리는 다가오는 자선 만찬 행사의 기업 후원자가 되기로 결정했다는 사실을 알리고자 합니다. 수익금은 여러 가지 암 치료 연구를 후원하기 위해 최근에 문을 연 노스캐이트 병원에 기부할 예정입니다. 주최측에서는 일만 달러라는 작년 기록을 깨기를 희망하고 있으므로, 모든 직원이 참석할 것을 당부 드립니다.

표는 일인당 40달러이며, 와인과 뷔페 식사가 포함됩니다. 회사에서 여러분의 표 값의 절반을 상환해줄 예정이니, 영수증을 보관해주시기 바랍니다. 만찬 중에, 화가들이 실시간 시연을 할 예정입니다. 그들의 그림은 만찬이 끝날 때 경매에 부쳐질 것입니다.

여러분은 이 행사에 참가함으로써 진정으로 다른 사람들의 삶에 긍정적인 영향을 미칠 수 있습니다. 질문이 있으시다면 언제든지 내선 29번으로 연락 주십시오. 감사합니다.

[어휘] supervisor: 감독관 announce: 알리다 beverage: 음료 corporate: 기업의 charity: 자선 proceeds: 수익금 donate: 기부하다 recently: 최근에 support: 지원하다 treatment: 치료 encourage: 장려하다 organizer: 주최자 reimburse: 배상하다, 상환하다 receipt: 영수증 auction off: 경매에 부치다 make an impact on: ~에 영향을 주다 take part in: ~에 참가하다 extension: 내선

55. 행사가 열리는 이유는?
① 회사의 최신 음료를 홍보하기 위해 ② 의학 연구를 위한 자금을 모으기 위해
③ 기업 합병을 알리기 위해   ④ 병원 개업을 축하하기 위해

56. 첫째 단락의 여섯째 줄의 'break'와 의미가 가장 가까운 것은?
① 파괴하다   ② 쉬다   ③ 멈추다   ④ 능가하다

57. 회람에 따르면, 행사에 등장하게 될 사람은?
① 무용수   ② 음악가   ③ 화가   ④ 사진작가

[58-61] (해석)

스핀마스터 드럼세탁기 관리하기

드럼세탁기는 조용하고 더 **빠르며** 물도 덜 사용하지만, 청소할 때 특별한 주의를 요합니다. 문 주위에 물이 새지 않게 고무로 밀폐 처리가 된 부분은 가끔 습기를 가두어 둘 수 있어, 이 때문에 곰팡이가 번식하게 됩니다. -[1]- 그러면 이 세균 때문에 세탁기에서 약간 냄새가 날 수 있습니다. -[2]- 아래 열거된 단계를 거치시면 이 문제가 해결될 것입니다.

1. 세탁기를 비우세요: 세탁기에서 의류를 모두 꺼내세요.
2. 고무 밀폐 부분을 청소하세요: 뜨거운 비눗물에 낡은 수건을 적셔서 문의 고무 밀

폐 부분을. 청소하세요.

3. 세제 주입구를 청소하세요: 세제 및 섬유 유연제 주입구를 닦아서 쌓여 있는 찌꺼기를 제거하세요.

4. 세척 순환을 작동시키세요: 세탁기 안에 식초를 넣어 빈 통 세척 순환을 작동시키세요.

위 단계를 정기적으로 따라 주시면 세탁기를 깨끗하고 냄새 없이 유지할 수 있을 것입니다. -[3]- 냄새가 지속되는 것은 세탁통 뒤에 곰팡이가 번식 하고 있을 수 있다는 뜻입니다. 아니면, 필터가 막혀 있을 가능성도 있습니다. -[4]-그러면 자격 있는 수리 기사가 와서 세탁기를 분해하여 청소해도 될 것입니다.

[어휘] care for: 관리하다 front-load washing machine: 드럼세탁기 watertight: 물이 새지 않는 rubber seal: 고무로 밀폐 처리가 된 부분 occasionally: 가끔 trap: 가두다 moisture: 습기 mold: 곰팡이 slightly: 약간 address an issue: 문제를 해결하다 soak: 담그다 soapy water: 비눗물 scrub: 문지르다 run: 작동시키다 pour: 붓다 vinegar :식초 oder-free: 냄새 없는 ongoing: 계속되는 indicate: 나타내다 clogged: 막힌 qualified: 자격 있는 repairperson: 수리 기사 take apart: 분해하다

58. 드럼세탁기의 장점으로 언급된 것은?
① 일반 세탁기보다 구입비용이 덜 든다.　② 세제가 덜 든다.
③ 세탁을 더 빨리 끝낸다.　④ 청소하기가 쉽다.

59. 냄새의 원인일 수 있는 것으로 열거되지 않은 것은?
① 문 주위에 쌓인 곰팡이　② 세제 주입수의 세제 찌꺼기
③ 막혀 있는 세탁기 필터　④ 세탁통 뒤의 곰팡이의 번식

60. 세탁기에 냄새가 나는 것을 발견하면 사용자가 가장 먼저 해야 할 일은?
① 스핀마스터 수리 기사에게 연락하기　② 세탁기에서 옷을 꺼내기

③ 세탁통 안에 식초 넣기   ④ 섬유 유연제 주입구 빼기

61. [1], [2], [3], [4]번으로 표시된 위치들 중 다음 문장이 들어가기에 가장 적절한 곳은?

"청소 후에도 냄새가 나는 문제가 지속될 경우, 스핀마스터 전문가에게 555-903-4862로 전화하시기 바랍니다."

[62-64] (해석)

시간제 운전사 구함

국내 최대의 네트워크를 가진 택배 회사 중 하나인 틸 사의 팀에 들어오세요. 우리는 신뢰도와 효율성에 대한 명성을 가지고 있습니다. 게다가 우리 직원들은 후한 복지 혜택과 뛰어난 간무 조건을 누리고 있습니다.

직무개요

선발된 지원자는 주택 및 상업 지구에서 소포를 배달하고 수고하는 업무를 맡게 됩니다. 교대근무는 주중에는 아침 6시 30분에 시작하여 대략 오전 11시 30분에 끝나며, 이는 그날의 업무량에 따라 그달라집니다.

자격요건
-최저연령 18세
-유효한 운전면허증 소지
-도움 없이 30킬로그램을 들어올릴 만한 힘
-종합적인 건간 평가 합격점수
-데이튼 시 구조에 대한 뛰어난 지식과 내비게이션 장치에 의존하지 않고 주소를 찾을 수 있는 능력

일자리에 지원하시려면, 애쉬우드 로 1679번지에 있는 본사를 방문하셔서 인사 담당자와 얘기를 나누십시오. 다른 공석을 찾아보시려면, www.thielinc.com을 방문하십시오.

[어휘] join: 합류하다 courier: 택배회사 reputation: 명성 reliability: 신뢰도 efficiency: 효율성 moreover: 게다가 generous: 후한 benefit: 복지혜택 position: 직위 summary: 요약 selected: 선발된 applicant: 지원자 drop off: 배달하다 pick up: 찾아오다 package 소포 residential: 주택자의 commercial: 상업용의 site: 위치, 현장 shift: 교대근무 depending on: ~에 따라 work volume: 업무량 qualification: 자격 minimum.: 최소 possession: 소유 valid: 유효한 strength: 힘 lift: 들어 올리다 evaluation: 평가 superb: 뛰어난 layout :구조 rely on: ~에 의존하다 navigation device: 네비게이션 장치 apply for: ~을 신청하다 headquarters: 본사 HR 인사부 representative: 담당자 browse: 둘러보다

62. 틸 사는 어떤 종류의 사업체인가?

   ① 택배 서비스 업체 ② 여행 전문 업체 ③ 공항 셔틀 서비스 업체 ④ 택시 회사

63. 일자리 요건으로 열거되지 않은 것은?

   ① 대도시 지역을 잘 알고 있을 것 ② 특정한 무게를 들어 올릴 힘이 있을 것
   ③ 유효한 운전 면허증을 소지할 것 ④ 주말에 자유롭게 근무할 수 있을 것

64. 사람들이 일자리에 지원할 수 있는 방법은?

   ① 지원서를 이메일로 보내서 ② 취업 박람회를 참석해서
   ③ 인터넷 상의 양식을 작성해서 ④ 회사의 본사를 방문해서

[65-67] (해석)

수신: 아샤 카푸어

발신: 해롤드 자일러

날짜: 12월14일

제목: 안녕하세요

아샤에게,

관심이 있을지 모르겠지만, 우리 회사에 웹사이트 디자이너 정규직에 대해 알려드리고자 메일을 보냅니다. 그 자리는 12월 20일까지는 공개적으로 광고되지 않을 것이기에, 당신은 이력서를 일찍 제출하는 이점으로 가질 수 있습니다. 패널 테크 사에서 일하기면 당신의 능력과 근면성실함을 직접 보았기에, 제가 기꺼이 추천서를 써드리겠습니다.

첨부한 것은 그 자리의 주요 업무를 요약한 것입니다.

필요한 자격요건을 충족한다면, 전 당신이 그럴 거라고 확신하지만요, 팀장과의 초기 면접 요청을 받을 것입니다. 그때 급여 및 복지혜택에 대한 설명도 듣게 될 것입니다.

지원하고 싶으시면, 인사 담당자인 레오나 애디슨에게 l_addison@bondsolutions.com으로 이메일을 보내세요. 그 과정에서 행운이 따르기를 바랍니다. 어떤 질문이든 있으시면 주저 말고 저에게 이메일을 보내주세요.

해롤드 드림

[어휘] full-time: 정규직의 be interested in: ~에 관심이 있다 publicly: 공개적으로 advantage: 이점 resume: 이력서 observe: 보다, 관찰하다 work ethic: 직업윤리, 근면성실함 firsthand: 직접 a letter of recommendation: 추천서 attach: 첨부하다 primary: 주된 initial: 처음의 benefits: 복지혜택 human resources director: 인사 담당자 hesitate: 주저하다

65. 자일러씨가 이메일을 쓴 이유는?
　　① 카푸어 씨를 면접에 부르려고　② 회사의 채용 공고에 대해서 말하려고
　　③ 카푸어 씨의 승진을 축하하려고　④ 지원서를 받았음을 알리려고

66. 자일러 씨에 대해서 추론할 수 있는 것은?

① 지난 달에 다른 화사로 옮겼다.   ② 이력서에서 오류를 발견했다.

③ 인사 담당자로 일한다.   ④ 예전에 카푸어 씨의 직장 동료였다.

67. 자일러 씨가 이메일과 함께 넣은 것은?

① 직원 명부 ② 추천서   ③ 직무 개요   ④ 면접 일정

[68-71] (해석)

인근 단체에 회의실을 개방합니다.

로즈데일 커뮤니티 센터에서는 정문 바로 옆에 있는 회의실을 무료로 다중이 이용할 수 있도록 지금 개방하고 있습니다. 회의실은 공공 단체 및 개인 누구라도 한 번에 최대 3시간 동안 예약할 수 있습니다. -[1]-

회의실 예약은 센터 안내대 에서 최소 하루 전에 직접 할 수 있습니다. 오전 10시부터 오후 6시까지 접수 합니다. -[2]- 예약 시에는, 신청서에 단체장의 연락처, 단체의 취지에 대한 개요, 예상되는 회의 시간, 앞으로 반복되는 행사인지에 대한 여부를 작성해야 합니다. -[3]-

회의실을 사용할 때는, 다음 규칙을 준수해주십시오. 첫째, 24명 이상이 동시에 회의실을 사용할 수 없습니다. 둘째, 뚜껑이 달린 음료는 회의실에서 허용하지만, 음식은 반입할 수 없습니다. 셋째, 사용자들은 떠날 때 회의실을 치우고 전등 스위치를 꺼주실 것을 당부 드립니다. -[4]- 이상의 규칙들을 어기는 사람들은 앞으로 회의실 사용이 제한될 수 있습니다.

감사합니다.

로즈데일 커뮤니티 센터

www.rosedalecommunitycenter.com

[어휘] neighborhood: 인근, 주변 front entrance: 정문 the public: 일반 대중 for free:

무료로 maximum: 최대 at a time: 한번에 duration: 지속 recurring: 반복되는 adhere to: ~을 준수하다 at the same time: 동시에 beverage: 음료 lid 뚜껑 permitted: 허용되는 restricted: 제한되는

68. 로즈데일 커뮤니티 센터의 회의실에 대해 언급된 것은?

　　① 하루 온종일을 예약해야 한다.　　② 업무용으로 만들어졌다.

　　③ 시간이 임박해서 예약할 수 있다.　　④ 무료로 사용할 수 있다.

69. 모든 사용자들이 회의실을 떠나기 전에 해야 할 일은?

　　① 음식물 쓰레기 치우기　　② 전등들 껐는지 확인하기

　　③ 회의실 문 잠그기　　④ 화이트보드에 적은 것 모두 지우기

70. 예약 신청서에 필요한 정보가 아닌 것은?

　　① 참석자들의 이름　　② 회의 시작 및 종료 시간

　　③ 단체장의 전화번호　　④ 단체에 대한 서면으로 된 설명

71. [1], [2], [3], [4]번으로 표시된 위치들 중 다음 문한이 들어가기 가장 적절한 곳은?

　　"취소는 예약 시작 시간 최소 두 시간 전에 해야 합니다."

[72-75]　(해석)

도서관 이용객들에게 알립니다.

베스트셀러 소설가인 도미닉 리마 씨가 저희 도서관으로 복귀할 예정입니다! 그 자신이 성공한 저자일 뿐만 아니라, 리마 씨는 또한 글쓰기 전문 코치이기도 합니다. 가는 지난 십 년간 세미나 및 워크숍을 통해 미숙한 작가들이 기교를 완성하는 데 도움을 주었습니다. 작년 이곳에서 그의 워크숍은 엄청난 인기를 얻었기에 저희는 그의 두 번째

귀환을 열렬히 환영하는 바입니다.

리마씨의 글쓰기 워크숍은 1월 24일 저녁 6시부터 9시까지 열립니다. 처음 한 시간 동안, 그는 소설가 지망생들에게 글쓰기에 대한 일반적인 조언들을 다수 알려줄 것입니다. -[1]- 짧은 휴식시간에 이어, 워크숍의 2부에서는 참석자들에게 자신들의 작품 일부를 서로 공유하는 기회를 줄 것입니다.

-[2]- 그 후에, 리마 씨는 참석자들 각각에 개별적으로 피드백을 줄 것입니다.-[3]- 이 행사에는 입장권이 필요합니다. 입장권은 앞으로 2주 동안 도서관 대출 창구에서 15달러에 판매됩니다. 직전에 오시는 참석자들은 워크숍 당일에 입장권을 수입할 수 있지만, 가격은 20달러로 인상됩니다. 그러므로, 반드시 입장권을 일찍 구입하십시오! 이 가치 있는 워크숍에 참석하실 것을 적극 권해드립니다. -[4]-

[어휘] patron: 고객 fiction writer: 소설가 professional: 전문적인 inexperienced: 미숙한 perfect: 완전하게 하다 craft: 기교, 기술 huge hit: 엄청난 인기를 얻은 것 aspiring: ~를 지망하는 portion: 부분 afterward: 그 후에 personalized: 개별적인 attendee: 참석자 circulation desk: 대출 창구 highly: 매우, 간단히 encourage: 권장하다 valuable :가치 있는

72. 도미닉 리마는 누구인가?

　　① 참고 열람실 사서　　② 유명한 소설가　　③ 책을 출간한 시인　　④ 문학 교수

73. 행사에서 진행되기로 예정된 것은?

　　① 소설책을 판매한다.　　② 참석자들이 서로의 작품을 평가한다.

　　③ 글쓰기에 대한 전문가의 조언을 공유한다.　　④ 다과가 제공된다.

74. 사람들에게 표를 일찍 구입하라고 권고하는 이유는?

　　① 행사가 가까워지면 가격이 오를 것이라서

　　② 참석자들을 위한 자리가 한정되어 있어서

③ 관심이 적으면 워크숍이 취소될 것이라서

④ 앞자리 표가 제일 먼저 매진될 것이라서

75 .[1], [2], [3], [4]번으로 표시된 위치들 중 다음 문장이 들어가기에 가장 적절한 것은?

"이전의 많은 참석자들은 이어서 자신들의 책을 출간하기 시작했습니다."

[76-80] (해석)

릴 투 릴 영화관 휴일 영화 주간!

일 년 중 그 시간이 다시 돌아왔습니다! 크리스마스가 다가오면서 릴 투 릴 영화관에서는 여러분이 이때를 맞아 질기시는 것을 도와드리고자 합니다. 크리스마스가 들어 있는 주 동안, 매일 저녁 여러분이 가장 좋아하는 크리스마스 영화 몇 편을 상영할 예정입니다. 오셔서 이 고정 영화들을 보면서 어린 시절을 다시 떠올려보세요! 관람 비용은 무료이지만, 저희가 지역 푸드 뱅크에 기증할 수 있도록 모든 관람객들께서는 음식물을 가져오실 것을 부탁드립니다. 모든 물품은 로비에 있는 크리스마스트리 아래에 두시면 됩니다.

저희가 준비한 영화는 아래 상영표를 보고 확인하세요!

월요일	화요일	수요일	목요일	금요일
12월 21일	12월 22일	12월 23일	크리스마스이브	크리스마스 당일
크리스마스 벨즈	특별한 크리스마스이브	올 크리스마스	베커 타운 크리스마스	겨울 소원
대표적인 뮤지컬 로맨스.	흑백 영화 코미디	한 특별한 소년에 대한 크리스마스 고전.	TV 드라마의 크리스마스 에피소드	유명한 소설의 네 가지 버전의 드라마

● 영화당 밤마다 오후 7시 30분과 10시에 두 차례 상영됩니다.

● 목요일이 상영되는 영화는 어른을 동반한 모든 연령대의 어린이들이 입장할 수

있습니다. 이러한 어린 관객들에게 부응하기 위해, 이 영화는 오후 4시 30분에 세 번째 상영이 있습니다.

<겨울 소원>이 없다면 어떤 크리스마스도 완전하지 않습니다. 그렇기에 저희는 이 영화만으로 하루 종일을 기획했습니다. 크리스마스 당일에 네 가지 버전이 2시간 반마다 상영됩니다. 첫 번째 영상을 오전 11시에 시작합니다.

[어휘] lead up to: ~로 향하다 re-experience: 다시 경험하다 classic: 고전적인 viewing: 관람 donate: 기부하다 food bank: 푸드 뱅크 iconic: 상징적인 dramatic version: 드라마로 옮긴 것. nightly: 밤마다 be accompanied by: ~을 동반하다 accommodate: 부응하다 complete: 완전한

수신:<info@r2rcinema.com>
발신: 유안 캐시디<cassidy@usermal.net>
날짜: 12월 27일
제목: 크리스마스 당일 영화 릴레이 상영

관계자 분께,

귀사의 크리스마스 영화 홍보행사에 대해 의견을 드리기 위해 이 메일을 보냅니다. 저는 12월 25일에 <겨울 소원>의 전반부 상영에 참석했습니다. 크리스마스 당일에 영화를 릴레이 상영한다는 아이디어는 정말 마음에 들지만, 그것의 개선 방법에 대해 약소하세 제한할 것이 하나 있습니다. 같은 영화의 여러 버전을 하루에 모두 상영하는 대신에, 몇 편의 다른 영화들을 관람하는 것이 좀 도 흥미로울 곳 같아서요. 내년 행사를 기획할 때는 이 점을 고려해 주시기 바랍니다.

유한 캐시디 드림

[어휘] lead up to: ~로 향하다 re-experience: 다시 경험하다 classic: 고전적인 viewing: 관람 donate: 기부하다 food bank: 푸드 뱅크 iconic: 상징적인 dramatic version: 드라마로 옮긴 것. nightly: 밤마다 be accompanied by: ~을 동반하다 accommodate: 부응하다 complete: 완전한 promotion: 홍보 suggestion: 제안 take A into consideration: A를 고려하다

76 .<특별한 크리스마스이브>의 영화 장르는?

　① 드라마　② 로맨스　③ 코미디　④ 뮤지컬

77. 관람객들에게 극장에 남겨줄 것을 부탁한 것은?

　① 기부를 위한 음식물　② 포장된 크리스마스 선물

　③ 입장권 구매 증거　④ 크리스마스 장식품

78. 목요일에 상영되는 영화의 색다른 점은?

　① 흑백영화로 상영된다.　② 유명한 문학 작품을 기초로 한다.

　③ 특별히 어린이들을 위해 기획되었다.　④ 여러 버전으로 상영된다.

79. 캐시디 씨가 이메일을 쓴 이유는?

　① 영화 상영시간의 변경을 권하려고　② 영화 선정에 대한 제안을 하려고

　③ 행사를 개최해준 데 애해 영화사에 감사하려고

　④ 극장에 두고 온 물건에 대해 문의하려고

80. 캐시디 씨가 영화를 본 시간은?

　① 오후 4시 30분　② 오후 6시 30분　③ 오후 10시　④ 오전 11시

[81-85]　(해석)

파인 패브릭 마켓—진구메, 시부야구, 도쿄, 일본

11월 15일

마누엘 산츠 씨
베스티지아 장식
올란다 3745
RM 뉴노아, 칠레

산츠 씨께:

희귀한 고급 원단을 판매하는 선도적인 도매상으로서, 저희는 자랑스럽게도 10여 년간 전 세계 인테리어 디자인 회사에 판매해 왔습니다. 그동안 인쇄물 카탈로그를 발행해 왔는데 최근 디지털 카탈로그로 전환하게 되었음을 알려 드리게 되어 기쁩니다. 디지털 카탈로그는 12월 초부터 이용하실 수 있습니다.

그때까지 저희가 독점 판매하는 주요 신제품을 소개합니다(견본 동봉):

"상승" (품번 462): 전통적인 디자인으로 서로 맞물린 사다리들을 연상시킨다. 광택이 있는 최고급 면직물; 파란색과 노란색.

"아침" (품번 517): 고대의 무늬를 토대로 한 이 디자인은 일출 시 산에서 올라오는 구름을 묘사하고 있다. 실크 다마스크; 흰색과 갈색

"원" (품번 614): 19세기 긴 웃옷 무늬에서 영감을 받은 둥근 꽃 패턴. 리넨; 보라색, 베이지색, 녹색.

"주기" (품번 628): 정교한 패턴으로 달의 주기를 연상시키며 기원이 서아시아라고 한다. 양모; 금색과 암청색

소중한 고객님들께 드리는 보너스로, 현재 특정 원단을 20미터 이상 주문하시면 15퍼센트 할인해 드리고 있습니다. 앞으로도 지속적인 거래 부탁드립니다.

켄타로 마나베, 영업부장

수신: kmanabe@FFMt.com
발신: msanz@vestigia.cl
날짜: 11월 20일

제목: 오늘 주문

마나바 씨께,

오늘 오전에 말씀드린 바에 따라 품번 462 "상승" 12미터, 품번 517 "아침" 26미터 주문을 확정하고자 합니다. 앞서 언급했듯이, 저희는 세 번째 원단인 "주기"를 고려하고 있습니다. 이 원단은 인기 있는 예비 의자 모델에 아주 잘 어울릴 듯합니다. 하지만 예전에 저희가 이 의자들에 천을 씌웠는데 찢어지고 해어지는 문제가 있었기 때문에 제 사업 파트너는 천의 짜임새를 우려하고 있습니다. 보내 주신 견본 천은 조금 작습니다. 가능하다면 저희가 천의 적합성을 결정할 수 있도록 이제품의 더 큰 견본을 보내 주세요.

마누엘 산츠

[어휘] fabric: 천, 원단 wholesale: 도매상 rare: 드문 decade: 10년 recently: 최근에 transition: 전환하다, 변천하다 available: 이용 가능한 swatch: 견본 exclusive: 독점적인, 고가의 interlock: 맞물리다 ladder: 사다리 polished: 윤이 나는, 광택이 있는 inspire: 영감을 주다 depict: 묘사하다 exquisite: 정교한 valued: 소중한 currently: 현재 confirm: 확인하다, 확정하다 order: 주문 mention: 언급하다 popular: 인기 있는 tear: 찢다 fray: 해어지다, 닳아지다 upholster: (소파 등에) 천을 씌우다 forward: 전달하다 determination: 결정, 판단 suitability: 적합함

[86-90] (해석)
'내추럴 펫츠'는 여러분의 애완동물을 위한 쇼핑을 간편하게 만들어 드립니다! 저희는 고양이 및 강아지 사료를 다양한 맛과 크기로 판매합니다. 여러분의 애완동물이 그것들을 좋아할지 여부를 판단하기 위해 여러 종류를 대량 포장으로 구입하기 보다는, 무료로 실험해 보시도록 해드립니다. 저희 홈페이지에서 선택사항들을 쭉 훑어보시고 테스트해보고 싶은 맛의 샘플을 선택하시면 됩니다. 직접 키우는 애완동물을 위해서 주문하시든지, 병원용으로 주문하시든지, 인터넷으로 주문하실 수 있으며, 다음 날 배송될 것입니다.

일부 고객들은 15% '단골' 할인을 받으실 수 있습니다. 할인은 적어도 한 달에 한 번 저희 제품을 구매하시는 고객들의 주문에 자동으로 추가됩니다.

[어휘] a variety of: 다양한 flavor: 맛, 향 determine: 판단하다 experiment: 실험해 보다 scroll through: 위아래로 쭉 스크롤하다 place an order: 주문하다 be eligible for: ~을 받을 자격이 있다 loyalty: 충실, 충성 automatically: 자동으로

---

www.naturalpets.com/shoppingcart

고객명: 아론 핀첨
주문 번호: 4354

제품	중량	수량	가격
내추럴 애완견용 - 칠면조 DF-535	4 lb	4	$128.00
내추럴 애완견용 - 연어 DF-576	샘플	1	$0.00
내추럴 애완견용 - 소고기 DF-642	샘플	1	$0.00
내추럴 애완견용 - 닭고기 PF-787	4 lb	2	$64.00
소계			$192.00
할인적용 (15%)			$28.80
Total			$163.20

수신: 고객서비스 센터
발신: 아론 핀첨
날짜: 4월 22일
제목: 주문 번호 4354

담당 관계자 분께,

저는 어제 주문 번호 4354 제품을 받았습니다. 저희 유기견 보호소용으로 일반 주문을

했으며, 몇 가지 새로운 맛의 사료를 실험해보기 위해 귀사의 홍보 행사를 이용하기도 했습니다. 저는 DF-535 제품 비용을 지불했는데, 상자 안에는 DF-353(양고기) 제품이 들어 있었습니다. 제품 번호가 매우 비슷해서 실수가 일어날 수 있었던 경위가 이해가 됩니다. 제대로 된 사료 봉지를 보내주시겠습니까? 또한, 최대 용량의 DF-642 제품을 보내주시겠습니까? 이 맛의 샘플은 여기 있는 강아지들 사이에서 최고의 선택이었기에, 그 제품을 더 주문하고 싶습니다.

감사합니다,

플릿우드 애완견 보호소
사무 관리자, 이론 핀첨 드림

[어휘] standard: 보통의 rescue facility: 구조 시설, 보호소 take advantage of: ~을 이용하다 lamb: 양 top choice: 최고의 선택 office administrator: 사무 관리자

86. '내추럴 펫츠'에서 고객들에게 하도록 권장하는 것은?
   ① 돈을 절약하기 위해 대량으로 구입하기
   ② 매장을 방문해서 주문 제품을 가져가기
   ③ 구매 전에 샘플 제품을 테스트하기
   ④ 최소한 한 달에 한 번 병원에 가기

87. 핀첨 에 대해 추론할 수 있는 것은?
   ① 특급 배송 비용을 지불하는 것을 선택했다.
   ② 개인적으로 키우는 애완동물을 위해 사료를 구입했다.
   ③ '내추럴 펫츠'에서 자주 구매한다.
   ④ 별개로 주 건의 주문을 했다.

88. 핀첨 씨가 추가로 요청한 사료의 종류는?

① 칠면조　② 연어　③ 소고기　④ 닭고기

89. 주문 번호 4354 제품과 관련된 실수는?

① 요청한 제품들 중 하나가 도착하지 않았다.　② 송장의 총계가 틀렸다.

③ 엉뚱한 주소로 배송되었다.　④ 배송 중에 택배가 파손되었다.

90. 이메일에서, 첫 번째 단락 다섯 번째 줄의 'top'과 의미상 가장 가까운 것은?

① 중요한　② 위쪽의　③ 최대의　④ 가장 좋아하는

[91-95] （해석）

빌브리지 미술학원 (BAI)

가을 강좌 일정

사진 기초 (오후 6:00 - 오후 8:00)	도예 I (오후 6:00 - 오후 8:00):
9월 매주 월요일	10월 매주 금요일
도예 II (오후 5:00 - 오후 8:00)	회화 (오후 6:30 - 오후 8:30)
11월 매주 화요일	12월 매주 목요일

다루게 되는 주제에 관한 자세한 설명은 www.bai.edu/classes를 방문하세요. 수강생이 용품을 구매해야 하는 강좌는 설명에 용품 목록이 포함되어 있습니다.

등록은 온라인과 방문 모두 받습니다. 수강료: 알곤빌 주민 125달러; 비거주민 140달러

---

http://www.bai.edu/reviews

처음에는 강좌에 등록해 금요일 저녁을 가족, 친구와 보내는 대신 도예 공방에서 보내는 것이 내키지 않았습니다. 하지만 카바니 씨의 수업을 딱 30분 듣고 나니 제 결정이 옳았다는 걸 알게 되었습니다. 유머 감각과 소통하는 강습 스타일 덕분에 수업이 정말 재미있었습니다! 작품을 하나씩 만들 때마다 도자기에 대한 흥미도 커지고 자신감도 생겼습니다. 실은 제 작품이 아주 잘 나와서 곧 있을 BAI 오픈 하우스 행

사에 전시될 예정입니다. 더없이 놀랍고 뿌듯합니다!

—멜리사 브룸필드

빌브리지(11월 21일)—빌브리지 미술학원(BAI)은 12월 29일 오후 5시부터 9시까지 연말 오픈 하우스 행사를 개최한다. 일반인은 센터를 둘러보고, 프로그램 참가자들이 한 해 동안 만든 다양한 예술 작품과 디자인을 감상하며, 수강생들과 함께 그들의 경험에 관한 이야기를 나눌 수 있다.

"우리는 15년 전 문을 연 이래로 해마다 오픈 하우스를 개최해 왔고, 매년 참가자가 점점 늘어나고 있습니다." BAI 원장 댄 프랭커가 말했다. "이 행사는 우리 수강생들이 재능을 보여 줄 기회가 될 뿐 아니라, 학원을 홍보할 좋은 기회입니다. 수강생의 정반 가량이 오픈 하우스 행사를 통해 우리 프로그램에 대해 알게 되었다고 합니다."

BAI에 대해 더 알고 싶으시면 웹사이트 www.bai.edu를 방문하거나 555-0147로 연락하십시오.

[어휘] ceramics: 도예, 도자기류 description: 묘사, 설명 registration: 등록, 신청 in person: 몸소, 직접 resident: 주민, 거주민 initially: 원래 hesitant: 망설이는 sign up: 등록하다, 신청하다 pottery: 도자기, 도예 decision: 결정, 판단 confidence: 확신, 자신 turn out: ~이 되다 feature: 특별히 포함되다 upcoming: 다가오는, 곧 있을 host: 개최하다, 주최하다 a range of: 다양한 participant: 참가자 attract: 유인하다, 끌어들이다 attendee: 참가자, 참석자 opportunity: 기회 publicity: 홍보, 언론의 관심 approximately: 대략

[96-100] (해석)

발신: 스베틀라나 리딕
수신: 마르첼로 로씨요
제목: 디자인 관련 내용
날짜: 2월 19일

마르첼로에게,

CR 465를 수정하면서 디자인 팀에서 몇가지 문제를 해결해 주셨으면 합니다. 우선, 오토바이에 대한 정부의 배기가스 규제 개정안이 이번 주에 발표되므로 디자인을 새로 변경된 내용에 맞출 필요가 있습니다. 또한 현재 모델을 타는 사람들은 후방 시야가 디자인의 단점이라고 말하고 있습니다. 이 문제를 해결하려면 거울 크기를 조정해야 합니다. 마지막으로, 2년이 넘은 오토바이는 칠이 바래는 문제가 있는 듯합니다.
디자인 단계는 6월 8일까지 완료되어야 합니다. 이번에는 마감일이 고정입니다. 제작팀은 지난해 대처해야 했던 시간과 예산 문제를 또 다시 겪고 싶어 하지 않습니다.
이런 유형의 오토바이 시장은 건실하므로 로드웰 오토바이가 평판을 공고히 할 수 있는 좋은 기회입니다. 이전 CR 465 모델과 마찬가지로, 경쟁사보다 가격을 낮추기보다는 고품질의 제품을 만드는 데 계속 주력할 것입니다.
감사합니다.
스베틀리나

발신: 마르첼로 로씨요
수신: 스베틀리나 리딕
제목: 디자인 관련 내용
날짜: 2월 20일

스베틀리나에게,

어제 규제에 관해 사전 통지를 받았습니다. 이미 오토바이 휠베이스 길이를 늘리려고 계획하고 있었는데 이렇게 되면 무게가 5킬로그램 늘어납니다. 새 규제에 맞추기 위해 배기 시스템을 바꾸면 무게가 추가로 5킬로그램 늘어납니다. 부드러운 핸들링을 원할 경우 무게가 총 10킬로그램 증가한다면 상당히 우려되는 수준입니다. 하지만 이 문제를 마감일 훨씬 전에 잘 해결할 수 있다고 확신합니다.
또한 번쩍이는 외관을 유지하기 위해 자외선 차단 기능이 있는 신제품을 사용하는 것을 고려하고 있습니다. 다시 연락해서 제조비용에 대한 제 견해를 알려 드리겠습니다. 디자인 변경이 큰 영향을 미치지는 않을 겁니다.

마르첼로

---

http://www.goroadreviews.com

짤막한 후기:

Roadwell CR 465

★★★★

이 멋진 오토바이 최신 모델이 10월 로드웰 오토바이에서 첫선을 보였다. 건조한 날씨에 탔는데 코너 도는 것이 부드럽고 정지 시 미끄러짐 현상도 없이 잘 달렸다. 올해 모델은 거울이 커져서 뒤에 오는 차량들이 훨씬 잘 보였다. 이 오토바이는 지난해 오토바이와 느낌이 조금 다른데 아마 무게가 10킬로그램 늘어난 때문인 듯하다. 로드웰에서 오토바이 트림과 핸들을 몇 가지 새로운 옵션으로 디자인했고 색상도 아주 다양하다. 가격은 지난해 모델과 비슷하다.

작성자 Tom333

[어휘] deal with: ~을 다루다, 처리하다 modification: 수정, 변경 emission: 배출, 배기 가스 regulation: 규제, 규정 address: 처리하다 rear: 뒤의; 뒤, 후방 visibility: 가 시성, 시야 weakness: 단점, 약점 adjust:조정하다 fade: 바래다, 시들다 manufacturing: 제조(업) opportunity: 기회 strengthen: 강화하다 reputation: 명 성, 평판 previous: 이전의, 과거의 beat: 이기다, 물리치다 advance: 미리 하는 weight: 무게 modify: 수정하다, 변경하다 exhaust: 배기 additional: 추가의 significant :상당한, 중대한 protection: 보호, 방지 radical: 급진적인 impac: 영향 debut: 첫 선을 보이다 perform: (자동차 등이) 잘 달리다 slip: 미끄러지다 slightly: 약간, 조금 weigh: 무게가 나가다 trim: (손잡이, 핸들 등의) 장식 a variety of: 다양한 comparable: 비슷한

저자 소개

박 현 석

약력
- 한양대학교 졸업(영어학 박사)
- 한양대, 광운대, 청주대 강사
- 현재 세한대학교 경찰행정학과 교수

저서
- Campus English(2001)
- 핵심수험영어(2040)
- 적중경찰영어2006)
- 파워경찰영어(2009)
- New 파워경찰영어(2011)
- 파워경찰모의고사(2012)
- 합격경찰영어(2014) 외 다수

핵심 토익 RC

초판 인쇄   2019년 12월 05일
초판 발행   2019년 12월 15일
저　　자   박현석
발 행 인   이범만
발 행 처   **21세기사** (제406-00015호)
　　　　　 경기도 파주시 산남로 72-16 (10882)
　　　　　 Tel. 031-942-7861, Fax. 031-942-7864
　　　　　 E-mail : 21cbook@naver.com
　　　　　 ISBN 978-89-8468-856-8

정가 18,000원

본 저서는 2019년도 세한대학교 교내연구비 지원에 의하여 출간되었음